EASY - MEDIUM
CROSSWORD
PUZZLE BOOK FOR ADULTS, TEENS AND SENIORS

This Book belongs to

TABLE OF CONTENTS

NOTES:

 Level: Easy

★★☆ Level: Medium

★☆☆

ACROSS

1. __ of measure (miles or pounds)
6. Vapor from a teakettle
11. "Let me think . . ."
14. Mount climbed by Moses
15. Pretentiously creative
16. Winning tic-tac-toe line
17. They buzz to wake people up
19. Internet address: Abbr.
20. Actor __ Damon
21. Brief in one's words
23. Strong grasp of a subject
27. Comes out of hiding
29. People playing roles
30. Decorated with blossoms
31. Sandals and sneakers
32. Old __ (American flag)
33. Software download
36. Clumsy one's cry
37. Gray stocking shade
38. Largest continent
39. At this time
40. Traditional Indian dwelling
41. Lazy __ (revolving tray)
42. Has the same opinion
44. Tranquil
45. Surprise greatly
47. Umbrella to block the sun
48. Treaties
49. Play friskily
50. "What did you say?"
51. What the other three long answers all are
58. What glaciers are made of
59. Wipe off a blackboard
60. Still sleeping
61. __ Moines, IA
62. Missiles thrown in pubs
63. In a grouchy mood

DOWN

1. Nation north of Mexico
2. Nothing at all
3. Once __ while (occasionally)
4. Goo for paving
5. Keeps just below a boil
6. Tasting like many pretzels
7. Jogger's pace
8. And so on: Abbr.
9. Inquire
10. Suspense novel
11. Sand-filled counters of seconds
12. __ code (telegraphy system)
13. Burrowing lawn pests
18. Sedans and coupes
22. Historical period
23. Bricklaying expert
24. Sound of a sneeze
25. Counters of seconds for races
26. Tips of slippers
27. Run off to wed
28. "The __ the merrier"
30. Chimney ducts
32. Stared with dropped jaw
34. "Baby grand" instrument
35. Group of experts
37. Adolescent
38. Eerie glow
40. Had confidence in
41. Tempter of Eve
43. Obtained
44. By the __ token (similarly)
45. Rosebush pest
46. Marinara or pesto
47. Finger jabs
49. Take a break
52. Keogh plan alternative
53. Scratch up
54. Edgar Allan __
55. Sci-fi beings, for short
56. Monotonous routine
57. Secret agent

★★☆

ACROSS

1. Session in the tub
5. Borders on
10. IRS form experts
14. Uncanny glow
15. Permit to enter
16. Noblewoman's title
17. Sound of scissors
18. Camel's South American cousin
19. Put __ appearance (show up)
20. Words to a pest
23. Tree that sounds like "you"
24. Something extra in an envelope: Abbr.
25. Tilt to one side
28. Poorly behaved
31. Robbery
35. Cheery greeting
36. Fold in a page corner
38. Formal neckwear
39. By any means necessary
42. Teachers' org.
43. Only just
44. Feels unwell
45. Continue until
47. Complete collection
48. Alphabet start
49. Distress signal at sea
51. Class for new immigrants: Abbr.
52. Proceed gingerly
61. High poker pair
62. Racetrack shapes
63. Stretched tightly
64. "You can say __ again!"
65. Variety show
66. Gumbo vegetable
67. Keyboarding mistake
68. What lumber comes from
69. Look intently (at)

DOWN

1. Low choral voice
2. Dad's sister
3. Quartet minus one
4. "Are you finally satisfied?"
5. Grant permission for
6. Strap around a waist
7. Nevada neighbor
8. Clock reading
9. Catch in a trap
10. Settle decisively, as a deal
11. Feeling of hunger
12. Eden guy
13. "Auld Lang __"
21. Wager
22. Start of a speech
25. Sparkled
26. Sheets, pillowcases, etc.
27. Still to come
28. Rude people
29. See eye to eye
30. Handed out cards
32. Moral code
33. Grassy land
34. Brief and to the point
36. Fabric coloring
37. "__ questions?"
40. "Are not!" response
41. Surface to set for supper
46. Invites out for
48. Campfire residue
50. Sound of scorn
51. Double-curve letters
52. Lightbulb measure
53. Sore from overexertion
54. Big jump
55. At any time
56. Donated
57. Arts-and-crafts adhesive
58. Canoeing locale
59. Entice
60. Have the lead role

ACROSS

1. Yuletide wise men
5. Helpful hints
9. Line on an agenda
13. Fathers of horses
14. Revered celebrity
15. Bend with the breeze
16. Makes preparations
17. Otherwise
18. Grocery shopper's sheet
19. Day early in the second month
22. "Electric" fish
23. Abel's mom
24. Sound of scolding
27. Weep loudly
29. Mistakes in a book
34. Exclamation like "Aha!"
35. Remove from office
38. __ boom (aircraft sound)
39. Day in the middle of the third month
43. Justice Kagan
44. Decade fraction
45. Spanish cheer
46. Anthem section
48. Young dog
50. "Permission granted"
51. And so on: Abbr.
53. Sample of a beverage
55. Day in the middle of the fourth month
64. Wild animal's den
65. Neighborhood
66. Egypt's capital
67. In addition
68. Con game
69. Bert's "Sesame Street" pal
70. (Had) observed
71. Servings of corn
72. Shut loudly, as a door

DOWN

1. Long distance for a runner
2. United __ Emirates (Mideast nation)
3. Any artistic category
4. Magazine editions
5. Level of a ballpark
6. Sit __ by (do nothing)
7. Pursuit group in westerns
8. Arm of a jacket
9. Spot of land in an ocean
10. Small bed size
11. Toward the dawn
12. Ancient legend
13. Sunblock stat: Abbr.
20. Uninterested
21. Poetry selection
24. Heavy books
25. "Thou __ not steal"
26. Seoul, South __
28. Harbor marker
30. Fish eggs
31. Pester
32. Name of a book or film
33. Has sore muscles
36. Seek damages from
37. Sandy golf hazard
40. Anderson Cooper's channel
41. Greenish eye color
42. Have faith in
47. Army "relax" command
49. Jigsaw puzzle components
52. Approximately, as seen before a year
54. Gem from an oyster
55. "That's too bad"
56. Drained of color
57. Stand up
58. Waffle __ (kitchen appliance)
59. Car transmission selection
60. Performers who overact
61. Ship of 1492
62. Quick haircut
63. Weed-chopping tool

★☆☆

ACROSS

1. Gets married
5. __ and crafts
9. Take a nap
14. Shakespeare's river
15. Any city with a harbor
16. Use a loom
17. State with Des Moines
18. Lion's sound
19. Taking a cruise
20. Material to knit with
23. Make a mistake
24. Tattle about
25. Sugary
27. "School of thought" suffix
29. Rented
33. "Gimme a break!"
37. Prefix meaning "all"
40. "Not guilty," e.g.
41. Destination for a direct deposit
44. Misplaced
45. Play friskily
46. Ham __ (sandwich order)
47. Chant heard at the Olympics
49. Segment of history
51. Swindler's victim
54. Draw out, as a response
59. Used to be
62. Upstairs area of a home
64. From Dublin or Killarney
66. Scent
67. Spill (over)
68. Taco chip dip
69. Greek cheese
70. Second to __ (the best)
71. Black hardwood
72. Went by plane
73. Approximately

DOWN

1. What a belt encircles
2. Bring to mind
3. Wooden rod
4. Slow-moving mollusk
5. Protective coverings for cooks
6. Top of a building
7. Meal holders in cafeterias
8. Scarecrow's stuffing
9. Southern river of song
10. Allow
11. Make simpler
12. At any time
13. Bartlett or Bosc
21. Computer printer problem
22. Artifact of the past
26. Touch lightly, as a shoulder
28. A third of tri-
30. Speak unclearly
31. Wee, informally
32. Palm tree fruit
33. Rights org.
34. ". . . but __ counting?"
35. Flat-topped hill
36. Misbehave
38. Studio with a lion mascot
39. Back of the neck
42. Very angry
43. Barbecue briquettes
48. Strut about
50. Sketch again
52. Sneer (at)
53. Alpine song
55. "__ big deal"
56. Hue
57. Smooths with steam, as a shirt
58. Universal donor's blood group
59. Using good judgment
60. Typical Saudi
61. Farm storage tower
63. Brief memo
65. Nine-digit ID

ACROSS

1. Free ticket, for short
5. Tenant-owned apartment
10. Seize suddenly
14. Milky-colored gemstone
15. Steer clear of
16. Capital of Italy
17. A __ pittance (very little)
18. Gave a fabulous review
19. Chimps and gorillas
20. Small dish for rolls
22. Duct for a clothes dryer
23. Houston ballplayer
24. Secret agent
26. Weep loudly
28. Banged accidentally, as one's toe
32. Playwright George Bernard __
36. Cash borrowed
38. Plank of lumber
39. Car with a meter
40. Of sound waves
42. India's continent
43. "__ you forgetting something?"
45. Ancient legend
46. ". . . the harder __ fall"
47. Cashes in, as a coupon
49. Large body of water
51. "__ whiz!"
52. Guiding principle
56. Fabric from sheep
59. Utensil for slicing sirloin
64. Soprano's solo
65. Row of bushes
66. Facts and figures
67. Movers' trucks
68. Raring to go
69. Low denomination bills
70. Animals with antlers
71. Garment worn with high heels
72. Desire to have

DOWN

1. Hair tool with teeth
2. Musical work with sopranos
3. Female horses
4. Fold of a skirt
5. Commuters' drive-sharing groups
6. Roundish shape
7. __ Scotia, Canada
8. Nutritional plan
9. Most peculiar
10. Vessel for pouring sauce on turkey
11. Tug-of-war cord
12. End of a prayer
13. Highest-quality
21. Physicians: Abbr.
25. London tavern
27. Explosive sounds
28. Grumpy moods
29. Lavish party
30. A Great Lake
31. WWII turning point
32. Hollywood headliner
33. Rabbit's relative
34. Chopped down
35. Goblet for Cabernet
37. "Pick a card, __ card"
41. Game with red and black disks
44. Golfer's peg
48. Fitted well together
50. Noah's ship
53. Establish, as a scholarship
54. Prince William's mom
55. Frequently
56. Hand-moving "Hello!"
57. Spoken aloud
58. Pig's sound
60. Rip in a fabric
61. Outer margin
62. Becomes more mature
63. Daybreak direction

ACROSS

1. Quarterback's throw
5. A bit less than a dozen
8. Dressed (in)
12. Muscle soreness
13. ___ de Cologne
14. Annoys
16. Start to melt
17. 24-hr. money source
18. Dip for taco chips
19. Farm bin for ears
21. Retained
22. Move like a rabbit
23. Hurry away on foot
24. "You, over there!"
26. Shape of a dollar sign
28. Vitality, informally
29. Bubble-bursting sound
30. Highway: Abbr.
31. Tire in a trunk
34. Fundamental
36. Feel poorly
37. Where a landline's handset rests
40. Display on museum walls
41. Puts in a certain order
42. Much-admired people
43. 3, on a sundial
44. "For ___ a jolly good fellow"
45. Roads that may cross aves.
46. Go bad, as fruit
47. Ready-made lawn
48. ___ Baba (40 thieves' adversary)
49. "Now I understand!"
52. Wipe clean, as furniture
54. Bottom of a freight-carrying vehicle
56. Notions
58. Edge of a drinking cup
59. Tortoise's race opponent
60. Larger cousin of a viola
61. Sixth sense: Abbr.
62. At the pinnacle of

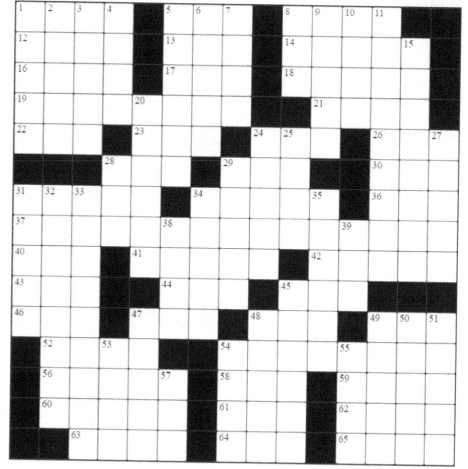

63. Whole bunch (of)
64. Crosses (out)
65. Baby bird's home

DOWN

1. Covering for a fabric hole
2. Sound of a sneeze
3. Good for cutting
4. Stitched together
5. Rip to shreds
6. Stay home for supper
7. Unable to feel anything
8. Walgreens competitor
9. Drippy, as a faucet
10. Auto's wheel bar
11. Old West outlaw
15. Wasn't fidgety
20. Moves on hands and knees
24. Tubes for vacuum cleaners
25. Long heroic tale
27. Tennis great Monica

28. ___-med student
29. Trousers
31. Walkway between floors
32. ___ table (chart of chemical elements)
33. Heights above sea level
34. Ready for something new
35. Writer of film reviews
38. Sounds from Santa
39. Billboard postings
45. Losing streaks
47. No longer fresh, as bread
48. Get out of bed
49. Lessen gradually
50. Long sandwiches
51. Expert (at)
53. Auction off, say
54. Fearsome dinosaur, for short
55. Genghis ___ (legendary conqueror)
57. Female pig

ACROSS

1. Colorado ski resort
6. Nimble
10. Feeling of amazement
13. Prolonged military attack
14. Earlier
16. Soup pot topper
17. Two-toned sandwich cookies
18. Specialized vocabulary
19. Raw metal in rocks
20. Box with aspirin and bandages
22. Barnyard cackler
23. Low-cal, on labels
24. Apple tablet computers
26. Daily print publications
29. Author Quindlen
31. Mobile phone, for short
32. Fruit-and-nuts snack
36. Neighborhood
37. Beef __ (dried meat snack)
39. Top-rated
40. Aerosol that repels mosquitoes
42. Argue the pros and __
43. Sailboat's pole
44. Light-colored beers
47. Mountain lions
50. __ and hearty (in great shape)
51. Find a purpose for
52. Roll-up bedding
59. Dog's hair
60. Deserves to get
61. Completely silly
62. Distant
63. Pig or hog
64. Painter's wooden stand
65. Crafty
66. Salty bodies of water
67. Slow-cooked meaty meals

DOWN

1. __ yet (so far)
2. Apple's digital assistant
3. Social equal
4. Swelled heads
5. Get cozy
6. Divides in two
7. Feeling of self-respect
8. Ice hockey venue
9. Cartoon bear or baseball great Berra
10. Hawaiian greeting
11. Did electrical work
12. Blissful locales
15. Corkscrew pasta
21. What fills an auto tire
25. Royal castle
26. Lima's country
27. Shake __ (hurry)
28. Type of flat-panel TV screen
29. Boat built by Noah
30. Negative Senate vote
31. Taxi
32. Give it a shot
33. Tie up at a dock
34. Rural hotels
35. Tic-tac-toe symbols
37. Eleventh graders: Abbr.
38. Have a meal
41. Free tickets
44. Runs out, as a subscription
45. Boxing great Muhammad ___
46. Magic-lamp occupants
47. Cream-filled pastries
48. Customary
49. __-go-round
50. Reddish hair dye
53. Legal regulations
54. A Great Lake
55. Pesky flying insect
56. Military outpost
57. For a second time
58. Types of toothpastes

★☆☆

ACROSS

1. Toward the sunset
5. Slugger's dry spell
10. Initial poker payment
14. Regulation
15. Copy machine powder
16. Light from a laser
17. Opera solo
18. Licorice-like flavor
19. Sentry's "Stop!"
20. Opening a champagne bottle
23. Eccentric
24. Neither here __ there
25. French-speaking Caribbean country
28. Periodical publication, for short
31. Unwanted breeze
35. Ancient
36. "Let me in!"
39. Fitzgerald of jazz
40. Making an angry exit
43. Ripped apart
44. Enters
45. Rowboat implement
46. "Stainless" metal
48. Attempt
49. Sentimental person
51. Beer barrel
53. Your and my
54. Playing a bongo
62. Rant and __ (show anger)
63. Baton-passing race
64. Lighten, as a burden
65. Colorful part of eyes
66. Brief moment
67. High cards in poker
68. Mattress holders
69. Freight train riders
70. Not as much

DOWN

1. Rolled-up sandwich

2. Coin in France
3. Lose one's footing
4. Vessel to brew pekoe
5. Get off a chair
6. Time-consuming
7. Self-storage rental
8. Netlike fabric
9. Fuss in front of a mirror
10. Detested
11. Very close
12. Have a chat
13. CPR expert
21. Figure of speech
22. Massachusetts' Cape __
25. Throws a party
26. Dole out
27. "Go ahead, __ you!" (verbal challenge)
28. Forget-__ (flower)
29. Feeling of fury
30. Full of nerve

32. Disinterested
33. Parade vehicle
34. Linger
37. Oinking animal
38. __ Beta Kappa
41. Timid nature
42. Happen next
47. One of a table's four
50. Difficult experience
52. Circumference
53. "Now I remember!"
54. With no decoration
55. Enthusiastic
56. Infamous Roman emperor
57. Smooth-talking
58. Folded Tex-Mex fare
59. Dash or marathon
60. Puts to work
61. Untidy spot
62. Part of a barbecued "rack"

★☆☆

ACROSS

1. Inquires
5. Girl explorer of cartoons
9. Squirrel snack
14. Took a photo of
15. Luau instruments, for short
16. AM/FM appliance
17. Rabbit relative
18. Envelope back
19. "That's yucky!"
20. Hardly __ (rarely)
21. Genealogical chart
23. Mystical gathering
25. Fasten securely
26. Antiquated
28. Pouch for pekoe
33. Up and about
37. Take a breather
40. Coke or Pepsi
41. False friend
44. Plumbing piece
45. Mediocre
46. Ancient man of fables
47. Incredible bargains
49. Good friend
51. Ins and __
54. Sheep sounds
59. Bill Clinton predecessor
64. Explosion sound
65. Removes the rind from
66. "__ put it another way . . ."
67. Suffix for luncheon
68. "There __ free lunches"
69. Close by
70. Slender
71. Soup utensil
72. Makes mistakes
73. Religious offshoot group

DOWN

1. Campfire residues
2. Remove one's whiskers
3. Seoul, South __

4. Back of a boat
5. Camper's bag
6. Tulsa's state: Abbr.
7. Packages of copier paper
8. Easy __ (simple)
9. Sock's diamond pattern
10. Grocery vehicle
11. Aroma
12. Get to one's feet
13. Carrot on a snowman, for example
22. Espresso with milk
24. Center of an apple
27. 007's first film foe
29. Farmland measure
30. "Constrictor" snakes
31. In addition
32. Inhale in astonishment
33. Snakes like Cleopatra's
34. Foul mood

35. Gift wrapper's adhesive
36. Scandinavian furniture chain
38. Sci-fi beings, for short
39. Compare prices
42. Topic for debate
43. Elaborate party
48. Connects to the Internet
50. Detests
52. Steakhouse order
53. More confident
55. Assists, as a criminal
56. Soak in the tub
57. Playful trick
58. Insurance broker
59. Nos. on college transcripts
60. Wyatt of the Old West
61. Black-and-white cookie
62. Nevada casino city
63. Top-billed performer

ACROSS

1. Happy cats' sounds
6. Mammals that fly
10. Armed conflicts
14. Sir ___ Newton
15. Help with, as a crime
16. Much-admired celebrity
17. Audacity
18. Lion's sound
19. ___ Scotia, Canada
20. Building for plant growing
22. Made a sketch
23. Camper's shelter
24. Made simpler
26. Skim some books
30. Poison-ivy symptom
31. German car
32. College official
35. Gem-studded crown
39. "Help ___ the way"
40. Fits of anger
42. Yale students
43. Tossed
45. Tiny bit of rain
46. Soft tosses
47. Taverns
49. Firstborn child
51. "Humble" residence
53. Lion's hair
55. Jogger's pace
56. Fancy lighting fixture
62. Injured
63. Toward sunrise
64. Long-winded
65. Brother of Cain
66. Sandal or moccasin
67. Wise saying
68. Walk through water
69. Hourglass contents
70. Affirmative replies

DOWN

1. ___-pong
2. Computer buyer
3. Highly uncommon
4. Rant and ___ (show anger)
5. Aromas
6. British noble
7. Approximately
8. Coffee alternatives
9. Urban road
10. Auto part above the dashboard
11. Like a lot
12. Wandered around
13. Cole ___ (cabbage dish)
21. Takes, as advice
25. Perform a role
26. Fishhook attachment
27. Go quickly
28. Aroma
29. Container for Champagne
30. Turn ___ (become)
33. Concludes
34. Balloon filler
36. Skin lotion ingredient
37. Barbecue orders
38. Helper: Abbr.
41. Pay out
44. Big bankroll
48. Courtroom break
50. Margin for error
51. Caribbean resort isle
52. Feeling ho-hum
53. Brick worker
54. Started a poker pot
55. Defrost
57. "That's funny!"
58. Vein of ore
59. Some tax-deferred accts.
60. Outer boundary
61. Sandwich breads

ACROSS

1. Office personnel
6. Staircase part
10. "Alaskan king" seafood
14. Bellhop's employer
15. Carryall bag
16. "Half" prefix for sphere
17. Nimble
18. Coupe or sedan
19. Tied, as a score
20. Pancake topping
22. Ladder crosspiece
23. Businesses: Abbr.
24. Texas city
26. Less risky
29. Like licorice or gum
31. Prefix meaning "against"
32. Factual
34. Eight-piece band
38. Performs in a chorus
40. Showery spring mo.
41. Weaving machines
42. Pebble or boulder
43. Passport stamp
45. Night-table light
46. Made simpler
48. Well-prepared
50. "You'll have to demonstrate"
53. Moral wrong
54. Sword handle
55. Guacamole
62. High hairstyle
63. Tip of the ear
64. Remove pencil marks
65. Move like a top
66. Like __ of bricks
67. So far
68. Earth-breaking garden tools
69. Borscht veggie
70. Valentine's Day flowers

DOWN

1. Deception
2. Garment of old Rome
3. "Take __ from me!"
4. Plummeted
5. Sheep's coat
6. Remains
7. "Guided" vacation
8. "__, Brute?" (Julius Caesar words)
9. Folks
10. Carbonated soft drink
11. Variety show
12. Modify, as a law
13. Game with numbered cards
21. Arrange into stacks
25. Military no-show, for short
26. Foul mood
27. __ time (never)
28. Bar-shaped cookies
29. Winged matchmaker
30. That woman's
31. Donkey
33. Rant and __ (show anger)
35. Frog relative
36. Television award
37. Sugar measurement: Abbr.
39. Stitched clothing line
44. Opera solo
47. Underwater research site
49. Make beloved
50. "Be quiet!"
51. Big African beast, for short
52. Any 1950s tune
53. Aroma
56. Mark a ballot
57. Woodwind instrument
58. Approximately
59. Calendar squares
60. "That makes sense"
61. Household cats and dogs

★☆☆

ACROSS

1. Foamy bar drinks
6. Tennis racket target
10. Do not possess
14. Tuxedo's collar fold
15. Soprano solo
16. Alda of "M*A*S*H"
17. "All kidding __ . . ."
18. High-schooler, usually
19. A few of
20. Fastest mover on a clock face
22. "Of __ I Sing"
23. Football six-pointers: Abbr.
24. Accomplishes
25. Size below Medium
26. Lions' lairs
27. 301 in Roman numerals
29. Convey, as wisdom
32. Employees learning the ropes
36. __ a soul (no one)
37. Churchgoing group
39. Salt Lake City's state
40. Animal shelter transaction
42. Opulent residence
44. Scallion-like veggie
45. Poker stake
46. Take it easy
49. Karenina of fiction
50. TV watchdog agcy.
53. Teheran's land
54. Time for the evening meal
57. In tatters
58. Meat inspection agcy.
59. Rich cake
60. Outer rim
61. Bottom-left PC key
62. Shoestrings
63. Crystal ball user
64. Tips of shoes
65. Apply, as effort

DOWN

1. Explosion
2. Made simpler
3. Heroic tales
4. Decorate anew
5. Slim
6. Soaks in the tub
7. Neighborhoods
8. Property claim
9. Touch down at an airport
10. Just before the deadline
11. Hawaiian hello
12. Beast with humps
13. Prepare to propose
21. "Tell the truth!"
25. Biol. or chem.
26. Schedule book
27. Bulky TV screen
28. Hot chili pepper
29. One __ million (rare)
30. Angry
31. Player who's paid
32. Soft metal
33. Incoming plane stat.
34. Have some food
35. "Steady as __ goes"
38. NASA affirmative
41. State south of Okla.
43. Scare suddenly
45. Historical records
46. Solemn ceremonies
47. Wear away
48. Size above Medium
49. Agassi of tennis
50. Compel
51. More adorable
52. Top of a wave
54. Ventilation shaft
55. "That's all there __ it!"
56. Elaborate deception

ACROSS

1. Wise person
5. __ Raton, FL
9. Taverns, and the theme of the puzzle
13. Backless sofa
14. 401(k) alternatives
15. Operatic solo
16. Motionless
17. Depend (on)
18. Crimson and scarlet
19. Little girls' plaything and girl-friend of Ken
21. Deep male voice
22. Take a chair
23. Train lines: Abbr.
24. Confident
26. For the time __ (temporarily)
28. Tasty tidbit
32. "Very funny!"
35. Geeky one
37. Garden tool for digging
38. Take __ (disassemble)
40. Get a glimpse of
41. Oxen harnesses
42. On the __ of (close to)
43. Sports squad
45. Glass in a monocle
46. Get larger, as a business
48. Butter-spreading utensil
50. Residents: Suffix
52. __-cone (icy treat)
53. Boxing match enders, for short
56. Adolescent
59. Liquid + whole-grain dinner serving
62. Typical Saudi
63. Jai __
64. Make really happy
65. "Yes! Yes!" in Spain
66. Sugar amts.
67. Made angry
68. Sharp, as vision

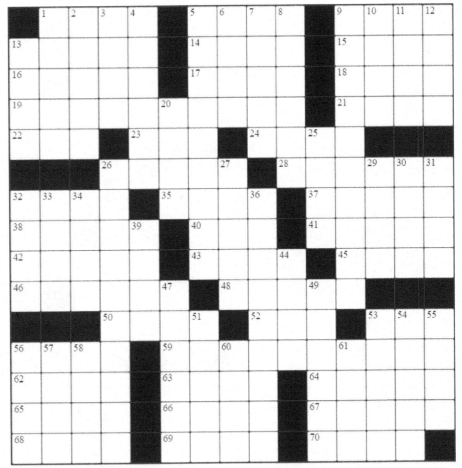

69. Toward the sunrise
70. Top-billed performer

DOWN

1. Ten Commandments mountain
2. Prevent from happening
3. Distinctive attire
4. All-inclusive
5. Home for eggs and hatchlings
6. Black-and-white cookie
7. Reaches via phone
8. Refugee's sanctuary
9. Old-time haircutter's symbol
10. Vicinity
11. Gets free (of)
12. Back talk
13. First claim, informally
20. Ireland nickname
25. Reddish, as cheeks
26. Store's discount display
27. Native of Athens

29. "For Pete's __!"
30. Biblical garden
31. A smaller amount
32. Be in possession of
33. Acme
34. Angel's instrument
36. Best-students roster
39. Camper's shelter
44. Underground gold source
47. Candidates' discussion
49. Entrance halls
51. Dip for tortilla chips
53. Bearlike Australian beast
54. External
55. Drove too fast
56. Job to be done
57. Small Great Lake
58. Alleviate
60. Knocks sharply
61. Cut in an envelope

ACROSS

1. Constructed
6. Sleep in a tent
10. Wagers
14. Winfrey of TV
15. Opera solo
16. Very hard to find
17. Oregon or Florida
18. On __ and needles
19. Neighborhood
20. Film's gown creator
23. Point opposite WNW
24. Family room
25. Show to a 72 Across, informally
28. In addition
31. Most confident
36. University sports org.
38. Lubricates
40. From then
41. One who chooses a film's actors
44. Female choir voices
45. Roll-call response
46. Ship captain's spot
47. Human beings
49. Football officials, for short
51. Highways: Abbr.
52. Pub serving
54. Sci-fi characters: Abbr.
56. Film's camera-crew chief
65. Black-and-white cookie
66. Melody
67. Felony or misdemeanor
68. Poetic daybreak
69. Biblical garden
70. Actor Costner
71. Concludes
72. Spot in the audience
73. Take care of

DOWN

1. Pear variety
2. Capable of
3. Keogh plan relatives: Abbr.
4. Espresso with milk
5. Uncle Sam's country
6. __ Canaveral, FL
7. Dry as a desert
8. Dug for gold
9. Free tickets
10. Boast
11. Be deserving of
12. Elm or maple
13. Scorch
21. Honeydew or cantaloupe
22. On, as a machine
25. Open up, as toothpaste
26. Weighing device
27. Must
29. Wistful sound
30. Born earlier
32. Well-to-do
33. "Come in!"
34. Give a reprimand to
35. Contract's details
37. Perched on
39. Kingly address
42. Religion of the Koran
43. Allude (to)
48. Makes very happy
50. Orders of pancakes
53. Piano practice piece
55. Shopping binge
56. __ in handy (be useful)
57. Clothes-pressing appliance
58. Geek
59. Ages and ages
60. __-day (vitamin dose, often)
61. Courteous fellow
62. Honeybee's home
63. Give off
64. Nevada city

ACROSS

1. $1,000,000, for short
4. Invoices to pay
9. Apex
13. Office helper
14. Spanish "So long"
15. Very slender
16. "Not guilty," for one
17. Use a loom
18. What's placed in a mitten
19. Driver's emergency illumination
21. Flexes
22. Has a hunch
23. Hourglass contents
24. Be able to pay for
27. Free tickets
29. Honeydew or cantaloupe
30. Signals, as a taxi
32. Attorney's expertise
34. Noteworthy deed
35. Overcooked
36. Female opera star
37. Physicians, for short
38. Tango or cha-cha
39. Kennel-club classification
40. Reduce in size
42. Rough, as sandpaper
43. Give temporarily
44. Give permission for
46. Go into a skid
48. Living-room illumination
52. Garment labels
53. Hotel room cleaners
54. Black-and-white cookie
55. Have sore muscles
56. Maxim
57. Camper's shelter
58. Software test version
59. Back-to-zero button
60. Feeling blue

DOWN

1. "Venus de __"
2. Notion
3. Fast driver, informally
4. Wept loudly
5. Absolutely perfect
6. Untruthful ones
7. Adore
8. U-turn from NNW
9. Capital of Greece
10. Ornate overhead illumination
11. Keep in __ (remember)
12. Concludes
13. First full spring mo.
20. Plant with fronds
21. Male singing voice
23. Pretzel topping
24. Two-band, as a radio
25. Serves dinner to
26. Theater usher's illumination
27. Tree with cones
28. Rescues
30. Thick slab
31. Rainbow shape
33. Walk through water
35. Small orchestra
36. Decide by picking sheets of paper
38. Have a formal meal
39. Mannerless person
41. Water that parted for Moses
42. Place to hang garments
44. Fake name
45. Skier's hotel
46. Wild guess
47. Shoestring
48. Become duller in color
49. Region
50. Patch up
51. Kitchen kettle
53. Scratch up

ACROSS

1. Open-handed hit
5. Toss
10. Spot of land in the sea
14. Money in Italy
15. Swiss miss of kid lit
16. Con game
17. Has a meal
18. Boca __, FL
19. Court order
20. Book jacket
22. Long-running disputes
23. Stage performances
24. Thick slice
25. Escorted from the premises
28. Student acquiring skills
31. Airport lander
32. Swoon
34. Sci-fi saucer: Abbr.
35. Otherwise
36. Ready for a nap
37. Hold firmly
38. Slangy refusal
39. Pigpen sounds
40. Theater walkway
41. Showed gratitude to
43. Sees eye to eye
44. Fortune-teller
45. Desert caravan beast
47. Had sore muscles
49. Finish quickly
53. Clumsy person
54. Very enthusiastic
55. Stare at
56. Ripped up
57. Farmland measures
58. Mined rocks
59. Drove too fast
60. Intended
61. Near-failing grades

DOWN

1. Sesame-__ bun
2. Hawaiian feast
3. __ and crafts
4. Reschedule for later
5. Where tonsils are
6. Hard to lift
7. Solemn ceremonies
8. Aroma
9. Be victorious
10. "Cross my heart!"
11. Surgeon's assistant
12. __-back (easygoing)
13. CPR specialists
21. Hint for a detective
22. Deflated tire
24. Mail away
25. Paid out
26. Islam's Almighty
27. Flow onto the beach
28. Isn't truthful
29. Pay taxes online
30. Tug-of-war cords
32. Locate
33. Noah's boat
36. Theater level
37. Females' youthful time
39. Approved of
40. Matures
42. Had to have
43. In the center of
45. Snake charmer's snake
46. Sci-fi being
47. Performs a part
48. Horse-hoof sound
49. Rate of walking
50. Fairy tale meanie
51. Make an escape
52. Admit the truth, with "up"
54. Lamb's father

ACROSS

1. Galahad and Lancelot
5. Portion (out)
9. Imperfection
13. American buffalo
14. Aroma
15. Shoe's string
16. Traditional Arctic dome home
17. Lima's country
18. At any time
19. "Ding Dong!" response
22. Healthful resort
23. Incoming flight guess: Abbr.
24. Diner sandwich initials
27. "O beautiful for spacious __"
30. Hatchlings' homes
35. Evergreen trees
37. Historical period
38. Last part of many plays
39. "Ding Dong!" response
42. In dreamland
43. End of big co. names
44. Extremely large
45. Puppies' cries
46. Walk inside
48. Crossed (out)
49. Unhappy
51. Tennis court divider
53. "Ding Dong!" response
62. Portal
63. Norway's capital
64. Angry
65. Woodwind instrument
66. __ opera (daytime TV drama)
67. Book of fiction
68. Give temporarily
69. Concludes
70. Impresses greatly

DOWN

1. Give an autograph
2. Castaway's home
3. Kitchens and dens
4. Is nosy
5. Sulk
6. Adam and Eve's home
7. Rich cakes
8. Spew 10 Down
9. Run away
10. Volcano outflow
11. Top poker cards
12. Used to be
13. Life story, for short
20. Mascara, lipstick, etc.
21. Jousting weapon
24. Less-traveled road
25. Tenant's document
26. Suit fabric
28. Tax collecting agcy.
29. Dine at home
31. Engrave with acid
32. Dakota tribe
33. Hint of color
34. Agreed (with)
36. Staircase part
38. Uphill climb
40. Old West outlaw __ James
41. Industrious insect
46. Light-bulb inventor
47. Eye part
50. Cropped up
52. Toss of the dice
53. Revered one
54. Tip of an ear
55. Lake bird
56. Raised, as racehorses
57. Feeling happy
58. Moves like a bunny
59. Roof overhang
60. Highways: Abbr.
61. Snakelike fish

ACROSS

1. Used a loom
5. Attended
10. Eject, as a geyser
14. Operatic solo
15. Without assistance
16. "Let's get out of __!"
17. Impolite look
18. High-calorie cake
19. Rabbit relative
20. Debate where voters ask questions
23. Cape __, MA
24. Surgeons' facilities: Abbr.
25. Makes changes to
27. Protection from harm
31. Strictness
33. Chicago airport
34. Speed contest
35. French friends
39. Mayor, council members, etc.
42. Changes the color of
43. Poems of praise
44. Decide to take part
45. Letters before tees
47. Things of value
48. Report-card marks
51. Rock that's mined
52. Fishing pole
53. Municipal building complex
60. Wildly excited
62. Quilt piece
63. Make simpler
64. "Absolutely!"
65. Happen next
66. Rock-band sound boosters
67. Appear to be
68. Beloved ones
69. Camper's shelter

DOWN

1. Disney of Disneyland
2. Black-and-white cookie
3. Point of __ (opinion)
4. Be worthy of
5. Overly diluted
6. Spiny houseplants
7. Arrange into stacks
8. Prefix meaning "against"
9. Adolescent
10. "No talking!"
11. War's opposite
12. Mistake
13. Plants pulled from gardens
21. Roadside stopover
22. Day-__ (fluorescent paint)
26. Vagabonds
27. Auctioned off
28. Sailor's "Hello!"
29. Clock dial
30. Removed from a blackboard
31. Rants and __
32. Puts frosting on
34. Went by bus or cab
36. Parcel (out)
37. "What's __ for me?"
38. Train stops: Abbr.
40. Repeated rumors
41. "Long time, __"
46. Fraction of a min.
47. Curved parts of feet
48. Lawn material
49. Scoundrel
50. Like a lot
51. Take place
54. Wind-direction indicator
55. "__ jungle out there!"
56. Well-groomed
57. Bring under control
58. TV sports channel
59. Take a break
61. Ruby or diamond

★☆☆

ACROSS

1. Folding bed
4. Shopping binge
9. Took a photo of
13. Dustcloths
15. Makes an attempt
16. Jay once of "The Tonight Show"
17. Cincinnati's state
18. Theater walkway
19. Shade trees
20. Dressy shirt-sleeve accessories
22. Plumbing tubes
23. Fruit-filled pastries
24. Fall behind
25. Vatican leaders
28. Unfortunate accidents
32. Yours and mine
33. Short putts
36. Country meadow
37. Sweater maker's implements
40. Earth-friendly prefix
41. Acquire
42. Very long time
43. Scoffs at
45. Gullible person
46. Maze-running rodent
47. Throw in the ___ (give up)
50. Hunter's wooden duck
53. They're worn when gliding behind a speedboat
57. Computer screen image
58. Kris Kringle
59. Bike's wheel
60. Sandal or moccasin
61. Large striped feline
62. Garfield's pooch pal
63. Grasp in one's hand
64. "Bedtime" tale
65. Nine-digit IRS ID

DOWN

1. Gator kin
2. Honolulu's island
3. Worker's end-of-week shout
4. Walkway between floors
5. Write with block letters
6. Takes a chance with
7. Snakelike swimmers
8. U-turn from WNW
9. Kris Kringle's vehicle
10. Lend a hand
11. "My treat!"
12. Easy throw
14. Most cushiony
21. ___ Vegas
22. Out of style
24. Fancy napkin fabric
25. Jabbed with a finger
26. Fraction of a pound
27. Earlier in time
28. Short skirt
29. Dole out
30. Rounded ends of hammers
31. Smart-alecky
33. Himalayan region
34. Picnic pests
35. ___ Tour (links organization)
38. At the present time
39. Provides with poker hands
44. Took creases out of clothes
45. Pay-___-view movie
47. Argentine dance
48. Playful aquatic mammal
49. Tired
50. Dinner plate
51. Repeated sound
52. A little chilly
53. Be patient
54. Youngsters
55. Eye-color area
56. Witnessed
58. Ave. crossers, often

ACROSS

1. Crown for a princess
6. Shut with a bang
10. Filmed, as a movie
14. Become inedible
15. Greek bread pocket
16. Exude, as confidence
17. "If only!"
18. Running __ (out of control)
19. "Once __ a time . . ."
20. Bearded New Year's Eve figure
22. Give temporarily
23. Take a break
24. Church services
26. Thorough investigations
30. Local sandwich shop
31. Prefix for circle
32. TV industry award
35. Religion of the Koran
39. Performed in a choir
40. Dalai Lama's land
42. Tex-Mex folded food
43. Big family, informally
45. Cape Canaveral org.
46. Reverberate
47. Peruse a book
49. Wild spending outings
51. Romp happily
54. Locale
56. Narrow cut
57. Rich source of anything
63. Elegant and expensive
64. Sandwich cookie
65. Comic-book punch sound
66. Poker hand starter
67. Leak slowly
68. Loosen, as a knot
69. Close by
70. Parts of a tbsp.
71. Annoying ones

DOWN

1. End-of-workweek shout

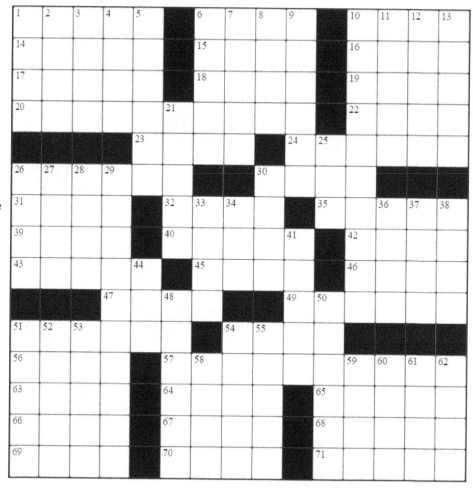

2. Des Moines' state
3. Very slightly
4. Reckless
5. Stick (to)
6. Minor quarrels
7. Place restrictions on
8. Molecule part
9. Schoolyard challenge
10. Woman's kindred spirit
11. Has aspirations
12. Atmospheric layer
13. Takes care of
21. Bowling-lane button
25. __ Baba
26. Whispered version of "Yoo-hoo!"
27. Bringing up the __ (in last place)
28. Prefix meaning "all"
29. Frat pledge's sponsor

30. Puts a new color on
33. Object to
34. Finance deg.
36. Shoestring
37. Charley horse
38. Sounds from cows
41. Fashion sense
44. Suffix for puppet
48. Not more than
50. Become more cheerful
51. Capitol Hill TV channel
52. Unaccompanied
53. Panoramic view
54. Having a sharp incline
55. Flapjack eateries, for short
58. Metallic rocks
59. Narrow road
60. Chooses, with "for"
61. __-yourself kit
62. Lambs' moms

Puzzle #21

ACROSS

1. Ginger cookies
6. River sediment
10. Hole-punching tools
14. Humble home
15. In the center of
16. Perfume bottle
17. Make amends
18. Traffic tie-ups
19. Turn __ (become)
20. Big name in motor homes
22. Luxury boat
23. Buy a pig in __
24. Soaks in the tub
25. Guys like Wyatt Earp
28. Thick soup
29. More frosty
30. Add decorations to
32. Female hog
35. Moral wrong
36. Squirrel snack
37. Make a knot in
38. Tack on
39. Comment from a canary
40. Insurance seller
42. Black-and-white cookies
44. Grocery workers
45. "That's life"
47. Pin the blame on
49. Vatican-related
50. Prepare for the cold, as a car
54. Memorable times
55. British chap
56. Italian salami city
57. Nevada city
58. Rocks found in mines
59. Is entitled to
60. Prayer ender
61. Exceedingly
62. Frozen precipitation

DOWN

1. Playwright George Bernard __
2. "It wasn't me!"
3. Shakespeare's river
4. Writer's alias
5. Convertible sofa
6. Pat of "Wheel of Fortune"
7. Public persona
8. Chauffeur-driven vehicle
9. 6-pt. football plays
10. Pilot a plane
11. Western rifle brand
12. Wood-shaping tool
13. Openings for coins
21. "__ voyage!"
22. Tall story
24. Catch fire
25. "Mona __"
26. Corrosive chemical
27. Glass sheet in a wall
28. Cruise stop

30. Highest poker cards
31. Female deer
33. Sound from a 32 Across
34. Moistens
36. Military no-show: Abbr.
39. Spill the beans
40. States without proof
41. "Be serious!"
43. Motive
44. Use scissors
45. Soap __ (daytime drama)
46. Sultan's group of wives
47. More elegant
48. Unable to sit still
50. Used to be
51. Memo heading
52. Urban district
53. Sunrise direction
55. State leader: Abbr.

ACROSS

1. Resorts with hot springs
5. No longer fresh, as bread
10. Surprise police action
14. Curved part of the foot
15. Yellow citrus fruit
16. Otherwise
17. Building's location
18. Licorice-flavored herb
19. Coke or Pepsi
20. Etiquette book author
22. Bellhop's employer
23. Rips apart
24. Not well-lit
25. Most meanspirited
28. ChapStick, for example
32. Above
33. Necklace fastener
35. __ tai (cocktail)
36. Essay in dailies
40. Poet's "before"
41. Serious-minded
42. "That makes sense"
43. Small rivers
45. Hay-bundling machines
47. Letters after kays
48. White-petaled flower
50. Warning signal
53. Santa's home
57. "Half" prefix for final
58. Reputable, informally
59. Region
60. Make docile
61. Self-confidence
62. "__ Sir or Madam . . ."
63. Aroma
64. Scornful expression
65. Mom's boys

DOWN

1. Postpaid envelope enclosure: Abbr.
2. __ and proper (overly formal)
3. First part of a play
4. Pet-adoption centers
5. Affront to, in headlines
6. Male singing voice
7. Out of whack
8. Misplaced
9. U-turn from WSW
10. Fix one's hair again
11. Frequently
12. Spot of land in the ocean
13. Distribute the cards
21. "Absolutely!"
22. Mudhole-loving African beast, for short
24. Hockey puck shape
25. Dog biscuit shapes
26. Keep from happening
27. Underground drain system
28. Animal fat for frying
29. Get a smile out of
30. More flimsy, as an excuse
31. Sources of coal
33. IRS-form experts: Abbr.
34. Luau necklace
37. Biblical hymn
38. 24-hr. cash devices
39. Frogs' pond perches
44. More spine-tingling
45. Tart-tasting
46. Fireplace residue
48. Cowpoke's stray calf
49. Stand up
50. Regarding, in memos
51. Be in first place
52. Bullets, for short
53. Store-sign gas
54. Black-and-white cookie
55. Tilt a bit
56. Portions of corn
58. Music recordings before CDs

ACROSS

1. Uneasy feeling
6. Rip, as paper
10. Evening, in ads
14. Calorie-rich cake
15. Rod between car wheels
16. Typical Saudi
17. Courtroom event
18. Borscht veggie
19. Elaborate party
20. One-person hotel room
23. __-Cone (summer treat)
24. Maze-running rodent
25. Tex-Mex dips
29. Camper's shelter
31. "You, over there!"
34. To no __ (useless)
35. Irksome person
36. Night before a holiday
37. Photos with ghost images
41. Saucepan topper
42. Dental exam image
43. Two hearts that beat __
44. Football field distances: Abbr.
45. 24-hr. cash devices
46. Explosions
47. Balloon filler
48. Boston cream or Key lime
49. Big bonus in Scrabble
58. Mystical glow
59. Long skirt
60. Lawn-cutting machine
61. Bring up the __ (be last)
62. Tied, as a game
63. Sports complex
64. "Over here!" whisper
65. Shipped off
66. Homes for hawks

DOWN

1. Lawyers: Abbr.
2. Formal "Me neither"
3. Wide smile
4. Male deer
5. Leaves no detail out
6. Prohibited thing
7. Corporate boss, for short
8. Actor Baldwin
9. Start reading again
10. Keep bothering
11. Teheran's nation
12. Bath powder
13. Online auction site
21. Junior naval officer: Abbr.
22. Portion of butter
25. Unhappily
26. Keep away from
27. Praises highly
28. Brother or sister, for short
29. Houston's state
30. Get a look at
31. Long sandwiches
32. Important happening
33. Affirmative replies
35. Long-lasting hairdo
38. Go to __ (overdo it)
39. Guy earning commissions
40. Nation n. of Mexico
45. Feel unwell
46. Auction offer
47. Take __ (disassemble)
48. Write with block letters
49. Waterproof covering
50. Feels regret over
51. Some S&L nest eggs
52. Water ridden by a surfer
53. Plow-pulling beasts
54. Center of an apple
55. Has bills to pay
56. Tenant's expense
57. Historical times

★☆☆

ACROSS

1. Flat-topped hill
5. Top poker cards
9. Being pulled from behind
14. Whitish gemstone
15. Start to melt
16. River of Paris
17. Be nostalgic for
18. Toon explorer
19. Pained expression
20. Well-educated
22. Prodded, with "on"
23. Lambs' mothers
24. Slangy refusal
25. Vegetable plot
29. Household rubbish
33. Light ___ (seemingly weight-less)
34. Give a high-five to
36. "___ the other hand . . ." (alternatively)
37. Glides on snow
38. Ejects, as lava
39. Very funny person
40. Money in Mexico
41. Durable hardwood
42. Bored by it all
43. Changed direction abruptly
45. Old Faithful, for example
46. Morning lawn moisture
47. University sports org.
49. Honey-colored
52. At an unhurried pace
57. Gets closer to
58. Solemn pledge
59. Region
60. Furniture to dine on
61. Suit to ___ (fit perfectly)
62. Flamingo color
63. Remains
64. Signals "OK" with one's head
65. Complete collections

DOWN

1. Female parents
2. Long, heroic story
3. Wide belt
4. In addition
5. When roosters crow
6. Routine task
7. British noblemen
8. Swing to and fro
9. "That's really the truth"
10. Helpful to those living close by
11. Sound of a small bell
12. "___ upon a time . . ."
13. Unwanted plant
21. Impolite look
24. Short snoozes
25. Sounds of fright
26. Out of whack
27. Salary increase
28. Untidy
29. Stare (at)
30. Opera solos
31. Honking bird
32. Walk inside
34. Drove too fast
35. Meadow
38. Slow-cooker meal
42. Boyfriend
44. Parts of poems
45. Deep cuts
47. Retro "Cool!"
48. Quoted as a source
49. Picnic pests
50. Veal or beef
51. "Ali ___ and the 40 Thieves"
52. Cash borrowed
53. Knocks sharply
54. One of the Great Lakes
55. Pre-Easter period
56. Chatters

ACROSS

1. Naval noncoms: Abbr.
5. Weighing device
10. Passed with flying colors
14. Absolutely engrossed
15. Immigrants' island
16. Evaluate
17. Black-and-white cookie
18. Long stories
19. Study hard
20. Jacket lapel flower
22. Artist Picasso
23. Foe
24. Karate cousin
25. Leave the premises
28.) and (, for short
30. Wise saying
31. Felony or misdemeanor
33. Had dinner
35. Tucker out
36. Dimes and pennies
37. Flower stalk
38. Lawn material
39. Small boat that's paddled
40. Vapor from a teakettle
41. Abs-building exercises
43. Barely at all
44. Grains in Cheerios
45. Fence post
47. Takes a survey
49. Craftsperson with wood
53. "Scat!"
54. Settle a bill
55. Former vice president Al
56. Give an autograph
57. Slight residue
58. Lose one's footing
59. Playthings
60. Pale-looking
61. Weeding tools

DOWN

1. Gator kin
2. Prefix for chute or medic
3. Switchboard worker: Abbr.
4. The Flintstones' era
5. Small couch
6. Insurance filing
7. Mix of metals
8. Legal claim
9. Letter before tee
10. Video-game parlor
11. Fizzy, as a soft drink
12. And others: Abbr.
13. Test-drive vehicle
21. Poker pot starter
22. Undiluted
24. Traffic tie-ups
25. Winery containers
26. Mexican "So long!"
27. Heart doctor's field
28. Tree with cones
29. Take without permission
31. Argue the pros and __
32. __ de Janeiro, Brazil
34. TV industry award
36. Baseball players' hats
37. Physical power
39. Uses scissors
40. "For Pete's __!"
42. Eagle's claws
43. Occur
45. Doctor's "open wide" request
46. Temporary peace
47. Attention-getting sound
48. Toledo's state
49. Theme of the puzzle
50. Matador's opponent
51. A Great Lake
52. Salespeople, for short
54. Grade-school auxiliary org.

ACROSS

1. Touch down at an airport
5. Synagogue leader
10. Did the backstroke
14. One frosting a cake
15. TV host DeGeneres
16. "Tall" story
17. "Guilty" or "not guilty"
18. Prince William's mom
19. Take a crack ___ (try)
20. Wave rider's platform
22. Apple cofounder ___ Jobs
23. Very nervous
24. Turned bad, as milk
25. Optimistic aspect
28. Extend a subscription
29. Big families
30. Weight-loss plan
32. "It's my turn"
35. "___ time, no see"
36. Rounds of applause
37. Winter precipitation
38. Total up
39. Annoys
40. Within the law
41. Pickling liquid
44. Cooks, as a turkey
45. Well-versed in a language
47. Standing tall
49. Shoestrings
50. Lightweight sphere tossed at the shore
54. Poses a question
55. Homer Simpson's wife
56. A Great Lake
57. "Now it's clear"
58. Used a crowbar
59. Isn't truthful
60. Goes bad, as an apple
61. Honking birds
62. Light browns

DOWN

1. "Read my ___!"
2. Legal rights org.
3. ___-do-well (rascal)
4. Choosing for the military
5. Decorated anew
6. Pen name
7. Loud noise
8. Flex
9. Buy a pig ___ poke
10. Sculptor's marble work
11. Tot's floating aid
12. Highly animated
13. Doled (out)
21. Cots and cribs
22. "___ of a gun!"
24. Full collections
25. West Coast school: Abbr.
26. Walk heavily
27. Container for seashells
28. Crimson and scarlet
30. Have the nerve (to)
31. Ballpoint liquid
33. "Billy" farm animal
34. Hooting birds
36. Clue
37. Car passenger's restraint
40. ___ Ness monster
42. Peanut-butter candy brand
43. Shoo-___ (sure winners)
44. Ebb, as the tide
45. Natural talent
46. Cowboy's rope
47. Hair-raising
48. Fits of anger
50. Unadorned
51. Soprano's solo
52. Property claim
53. Not so much
55. Fuel efficiency stat.

ACROSS

1. Run leisurely
5. Lasting mark
9. Barber's sharpener
14. Astronauts' agcy.
15. Prepare to be photographed
16. Wear away
17. Cash drawer
18. Totally wreck
19. Stay home for supper
20. Where to wait for a flu shot
23. Crude shelter
24. Liquid for frying
25. Gets the job done, informally
29. Performer's role
31. Taking a vacation day
34. Very pale
35. Small town
36. Wise advisor
37. Where to wait to pay for groceries
40. Exam
41. Barracks beds
42. Breakfast roll with a hole
43. Anger
44. Shoreline indentations
45. Engines
46. "You've got mail" Web company
47. Briny body of water
48. Where to wait for an underground train
55. Man-made waterway
56. Apple tablet computer
57. Eject, as a geyser
59. Licorice-flavored herb
60. Sport on horseback
61. Not on time
62. Try to prevent
63. Meat + potatoes dish
64. Otherwise

DOWN

1. Blasting material: Abbr.

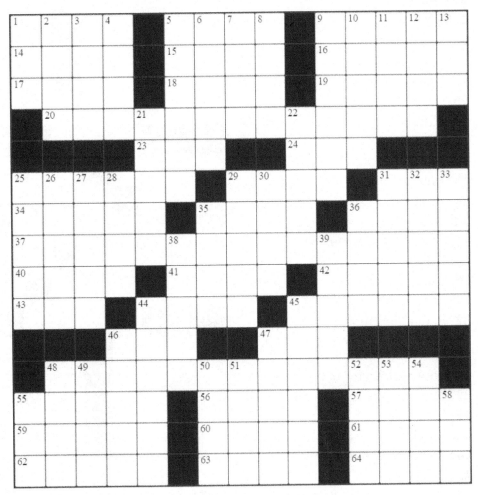

2. Sudden police action
3. Capital of Norway
4. Bath powder
5. Start to blossom
6. Judge's workplace
7. With no warranty
8. Nevada casino city
9. Believe appropriate
10. Hiking path
11. College military grp.
12. Garfield's pooch pal
13. Ballpoint
21. "Use your head!"
22. Do without
25. Spiny desert plants
26. Theater employee
27. One of __ days (eventually)
28. Splinter group
29. Hole-finishing golf strokes
30. Curved lines

31. Money spent
32. Less restrained
33. Rolls up, as a flag
35. Floating harbor marker
36. Pesky flying insect
38. City near Orlando
39. WWII sub
44. One scoring strikes and spares
45. Grassy field
46. Belittle
47. Not fresh, as bread
48. Rational
49. __ of measure (mile or quart)
50. Puppy sounds
51. Catch sight of
52. Land surrounded by water
53. Whitish gemstone
54. Table tennis dividers
55. Unmannerly guy
58. Very small

ACROSS

1. Prods into action
6. Drains of energy
10. Junk email
14. Of eyesight
15. Luau dance
16. Manage somehow
17. Turn loose
18. Word-of-mouth
19. Pub beverages
20. Skillets for sautéing
22. Soft throw
23. Coffee alternative
24. Pretzel topping
26. Settles a bill
29. Bar bill, informally
32. Feel inner anger
36. Urban rd. that might cross a street
37. Thorny flowers
39. Battleship colors
40. Mac-and-cheese containers
43. Small hill
44. Group of battleships
45. Dollar bill
46. Small river
48. Sixth sense, for short
49. Salty bodies of water
50. Corporate VIP
52. Fill in __ blank
54. Novel or biography
57. Pots for cooking stews
63. One of the Great Lakes
64. Region
65. Wigwam cousin
66. Snakelike swimmers
67. Isn't truthful
68. Build, as a house
69. Fence stake
70. __ of the time (now and then)
71. Onionlike veggies

DOWN

1. Sport with fairways and greens
2. Letters on a phone's "0" button
3. Lawyer: Abbr.
4. Numbers from 0 to 9
5. Pastry served with 23 Across
6. Compare prices
7. Mystical glow
8. Makes preparations
9. Tex-Mex dips
10. Strews about
11. Sport on horseback
12. Gorillas and chimps
13. Untidiness
21. Croc's cousin
25. Reputable
26. Fills a suitcase
27. __-garde (stylishly bold)
28. "__ no?" (simple question)
30. Beginning from
31. Charming southern woman
33. Nevada resort lake
34. "Laughing" African beast
35. Letters before tees
37. Take a break
38. Glimpses
41. Most smooth and stylish
42. Distance below the surface
47. Olympic prizes
49. Harsh in manner
51. Unusual collectible
53. Bellhop's employer
54. Microwave oven sound
55. Black-and-white cookie
56. Lubricates
58. Be abundant
59. Job for a detective
60. Fencing sword
61. Giraffe's notable feature
62. Full collections

Puzzle #29

29

ACROSS

1. Catch a glimpse of
5. Diamonds and rubies
9. Pizza's outer rim
14. Volcano outflow
15. Garfield's canine friend
16. Charged towards
17. Whitish birthstone
18. Despicable
19. Find the sum of
20. Posters and murals
23. Sculpture or painting
24. Chinese restaurant beverage
25. Pack tightly
29. __ Moines, IA
31. Cash advance
35. Mystical glows
36. Wise ones
38. Metallic rock
39. Shoe rack or garment rack
42. Garment edge
43. Sandals and sneakers
44. For days __ (continuously)
45. Memorable time periods
47. Part of TGIF
48. Start of many workweeks
49. Anderson Cooper's network
51. Young dog
52. Xbox or PlayStation
61. Native of Teheran
62. Atlas pages
63. Keep out of sight
64. Puts in alphabetical order
65. Otherwise
66. Colored part of the eye
67. Fidgety
68. Astronaut Armstrong
69. Parakeets and poodles

DOWN

1. Reduce one's speed
2. Biggest of the Three Bears
3. Egg-shaped
4. Above average in height
5. Run a country
6. Royal decree
7. "Venus de __"
8. Fortune-teller
9. Box for oranges
10. With 58 Down, type of auto wheel
11. Loosen, as laces
12. Astonish
13. Spinning toys
21. Banquet platforms
22. On a cruise
25. Hidden supply
26. Measuring stick
27. Fragrance
28. Mothers, informally
29. Takes a risk
30. They're cracked for omelets
32. Seeped
33. Sports or concert venue
34. Not at all hip
36. Chimney dust
37. Charlie Brown's dog
40. Inanimate object
41. Quaint hotel
46. Fragrances
48. Oyster's cousin
50. Too loud
51. Coca-Cola competitor
52. Border-crossing document
53. Clothes-pressing appliance
54. Pub-game missile
55. Prayer ending
56. Rooster or ram
57. Ocean vessel
58. See 10 Down
59. Spruce up, as an essay
60. Untidy condition

ACROSS

1. Tiny, pesky flies
6. Prepare for a bout
10. Bowling alley targets
14. Fastener in a girder
15. Give as an example
16. Notion
17. Being chilled, as champagne
18. Very much
19. Applaud
20. Worry-free felt-tip pens
23. Accomplished
24. Wall-climbing plant
25. Of odes and sonnets
29. Buddies
31. 24-hr. bank device
34. Chicago airport
35. Husband or wife
36. Model builder's adhesive
37. Worry-free liquid for a tot's art-work
40. A Great Lake
41. Highway exit
42. Banquet host
43. Was in charge of
44. Uses scissors
45. War horses
46. Point at a target
47. Moral wrong
48. Worry-free coloring-book imple-ments
57. Don't have
58. Entice
59. __ Antoinette (French queen)
60. Silent performer
61. Deserve
62. Make very happy
63. Snow vehicle
64. Covering on attic items
65. Tennis great Monica

DOWN

1. Get taller

2. One of Columbus' ships
3. Hertz rival
4. Computer support person
5. Less wobbly
6. Burn with hot liquid
7. Stack
8. Molecule part
9. Store merchant
10. Overly fussy
11. Not doing anything
12. Close by
13. Drains of energy
21. Paper Mate competitor
22. Campers' vehicles, for short
25. Electricity supply
26. Scarlett of "Gone With the Wind"
27. Have dinner at home
28. Family __ (genealogy chart)
29. Coconut sources
30. Perched on

31. Wonderland girl
32. Adjusted, as a guitar
33. Parcels (out)
35. Water around a castle
36. Scrabble or Monopoly
38. Broke into little pieces
39. Terms of affection
44. US spy org.
45. Knight's title
46. Posed a question
47. Aroma
48. Shade sources
49. Staircase banister
50. Apex
51. Hawaiian cookout
52. Makes a mistake
53. New Haven university
54. Taken by mouth
55. Evening, in ads
56. Gets a glimpse of

ACROSS

1. Taxis
5. Soccer score
9. Canoes and kayaks
14. All over again
15. Not doing anything
16. Regions
17. River through Egypt
18. __ Scotia, Canada
19. Second showing on TV
20. Spot of land in the sea
21. Political support of regular people
23. Acquire molars and canines
25. Fill in __ blank
26. Makes mistakes
29. "Same with me!"
34. Copy-machine powder
38. Organization for people 50+
40. In __ (lined up)
41. Yale or Princeton
44. Weather report charts
45. Look after
46. Coupes and convertibles
47. Firstborn child
49. Right away, in memos
51. That man's
53. Sight and smell
58. Sailors' short coats
64. Unwrap, as a gift
65. Misbehave
66. Sudden impulse
67. Bike's wheel
68. Lamp covering
69. "Tender" beef cut
70. One of the Great Lakes
71. Commotions
72. Barn's upper level
73. Fortune-teller

DOWN

1. "Be quiet!"
2. Licorice-flavored herb
3. Charming Southern woman
4. Sugary
5. __ snap (type of cookie)
6. Scent
7. Thomas __ Edison
8. Minimum amount
9. Kept from entering
10. Black-and-white cookie
11. Aviation-related prefix
12. Tightly stretched
13. Tax form IDs
22. Ocean vessels
24. Roll-call response
27. Intense anger
28. Steam room
30. Honolulu's island
31. Jogger's pace
32. Trip odometer's initial reading
33. "Wise" birds
34. Clock reading
35. Shape of an egg
36. Big Apple cops' org.
37. Otherwise
39. Crimson and scarlet
42. Home's upper storage area
43. __ Cod, MA
48. Circles and triangles
50. Agree (to)
52. __ and crossbones (pirate flag)
54. Brief memos
55. Church steeple
56. Spooky
57. Scornful expression
58. In the __ (long ago)
59. Canyon sound
60. Just slightly
61. Japanese martial art
62. Slangy suffix for switch
63. Employee's end-of-week shout

Puzzle #32

ACROSS

1. Dishonest imitation
5. Person walking in a pond
10. Highway exit
14. ___ colada (cocktail)
15. Stick out like ___ thumb
16. One of the Great Lakes
17. Omelet ingredients
18. Made furious
19. Clothes-dryer fuzz
20. Competition with kings and rooks
22. Calculates a total
23. French-style pancake
24. Broadway show award
26. Helper: Abbr.
29. Plaid kilt pattern
33. Break sharply
37. Small fruit pie
39. Marinara or pesto
40. Turn on one foot
42. "Dear ___ or Madam . . ."
43. Farmland measures
44. "Great minds think ___"
45. Fortune-teller
47. Concludes
48. Deal in secondhand goods
50. Doe or fawn
52. Sit down with a book
54. Hope-chest wood
58. Thick carpet
61. Boxing competition
65. Heavy marching-band instrument
66. Removed the center of, as apples
67. Scenic sight
68. Grad
69. Licorice-flavored herb
70. Female singing voice
71. Fence opening
72. Midterms and finals
73. Complete collections

DOWN

1. Blueprint detail, for short
2. Soprano's note
3. Enrage
4. En ___ (as a group)
5. Most friendly
6. India's continent
7. Foolish person
8. Build, as a house
9. Very spicy
10. Baton-passing track competition
11. Dry as a desert
12. Keep in ___ (remember)
13. Parakeets and poodles
21. Resort with hot springs
25. Astronauts' agcy.
27. Talk back to
28. Made an attempt
30. Go right or left
31. Scored 100 percent on
32. Loch ___ monster
33. Practice for a 61 Across
34. Long river ending in Egypt
35. Hertz competitor
36. Competition with straights and flushes
38. Elm or maple
41. Prefix for vision or scope
46. Ebbs
49. Cuddly, purring animal
51. Touchdown caller, for short
53. Plane without a pilot
55. Female opera stars
56. Well-coordinated
57. Butler of "Gone With the Wind"
58. Guys-only event
59. Luau dance
60. Border on
62. Colored part of the eye
63. Enthusiasm
64. Lowest pair in a 36 Down

ACROSS

1. Top of the head
6. Sugar amts.
10. Crunchy sandwiches, for short
14. Cloth for drying
15. Take a crack ___ (try)
16. Very funny person
17. Sports venue
18. Da Vinci's "___ Lisa"
19. Not fooled by
20. Fish entrée
22. Erode
23. Historical periods
24. Light on a birthday cake
26. Railroad stations
30. Thick carpet
31. Aroma
32. Black-and-white cookie
35. Have a quarrel
39. One of Columbus' ships
40. Twangy, as a voice
42. ___-Seltzer (antacid brand)
43. Shorthand expert
45. Lap dog, for short
46. Neckline shapes
47. Burst of wind
49. Most desertlike
51. Photographic device
54. Destiny
56. Letters meaning "Pronto!"
57. Side dish on a cob
63. Get weary
64. Slanted typeface: Abbr.
65. Song from the '60s, say
66. Outer margin
67. Nominate
68. Midnight fridge visits
69. Fishing line holder
70. Small valley
71. Joints above ankles

DOWN

1. Top-billed actor
2. Apple's center
3. More than impressed
4. See-through part of a 51 Across
5. Venus or Mars
6. Western Florida city
7. Halts
8. Cone-bearing tree
9. Shirt stiffener
10. Sauce for mashed potatoes
11. ___ up (in a queue)
12. Bottom-line figure
13. Mall tenant
21. Fire-setting felony
25. Motorists' org.
26. Puts on, as clothing
27. Polish, as a manuscript
28. Southern cornbread
29. Marmalade ingredient
30. Drench
33. Fully attentive
34. Point opposite WNW
36. Happy feeling
37. Luau instruments, for short
38. Sunrise direction
41. Resulted in
44. Belonging to us
48. Uttering
50. Try again with, as a manuscript
51. Provide food for a banquet
52. "All kidding ___ . . ."
53. Homer Simpson's wife
54. Top of a 24 Across
55. Director Woody
58. And others: Abbr.
59. Big family
60. Garfield's canine friend
61. Ferris wheel or roller coaster
62. Loch ___ monster

ACROSS

1. White sandwich spread, for short
5. Eject, as lava
9. Paper fragment
14. Pub beverages
15. Low female voice
16. Nickels and quarters
17. Breakfast or dinner
18. Gooey dirt
19. Evicts
20. Really nearby
23. Pigeon sound
24. Part of TGIF
25. Meshy window insert
29. Young boy
31. Flightless Aussie birds
35. Martian, for example
36. Simplifies
38. Stamp-pad fluid
39. Really nearby
42. Intense anger
43. Chills down
44. Banish
45. Thumbs-down Senate votes
47. Compass point opposite NNW
48. Arrange in advance
49. Coconut custard __
51. Tic-tac-__
52. Really nearby
61. Lacked, informally
62. Sergeant or captain
63. Sedan or coupe
64. Draw out, as memories
65. Spiny houseplant
66. Happy
67. Actress Streep
68. Any town with a harbor
69. Otherwise

DOWN

1. Papa's partner
2. Actor Baldwin
3. January through December
4. Norway's capital
5. Biblical strongman
6. Dwarf planet beyond Neptune
7. Engrave with acid
8. Roused from sleep
9. Francis __ Key
10. Place to play golf
11. Stand up
12. Initial poker payment
13. "Hey, you!"
21. Picturesque
22. Two __ to every story
25. Welcomed through the door
26. Barton of the Red Cross
27. Life of __ (carefree existence)
28. "A mouse!"
29. Soup-serving utensil
30. With no warranty
32. Short skirts
33. Dad's brother
34. Sport with clay pigeons
36. Swelled heads
37. Two-speaker sound system
40. Snooped (around)
41. Tree-chopping tool
46. Courageous and determined
48. Pool-table hole
50. Info gathered by spies
51. High male voice
52. Throat-clearing sound
53. Four-star review
54. Aroma
55. Sandy golf hazard
56. Angel's topper
57. Intense anger
58. __ and void (not valid)
59. When planes are due in: Abbr.
60. Was a passenger

ACROSS

1. Catch sight of
5. High-school dances
10. Long heroic story
14. Volcano's outflow
15. One of the Great Lakes
16. Highway pathway
17. Gorillas and chimps
18. Basketball great Shaquille
19. Paid athletes
20. Office cubicle divider
22. "In case you __ noticed . . ."
23. Clickable computer images
24. Coin in Mexico
25. Wigwam relatives
28. Is a member
31. Accumulate
32. Caught sight of
34. Once and for __ (permanently)
35. Supermarket vehicle
36. Sewing-thread holder
37. Woodwind instrument
38. Liquid for frying
39. Watermelon discards
40. Heartbeat
41. Lost traction on ice
43. Loathe
44. Grad at a reunion
45. Take illegally
47. Wanderer
49. 40 Down "tree" bird in a Christmas carol
53. Biblical garden
54. Adorable toddler
55. Christmas carol
56. Napa Valley beverage
57. Not as humid
58. Makes mistakes
59. Complete collections
60. Drops in a mailbox
61. Identical

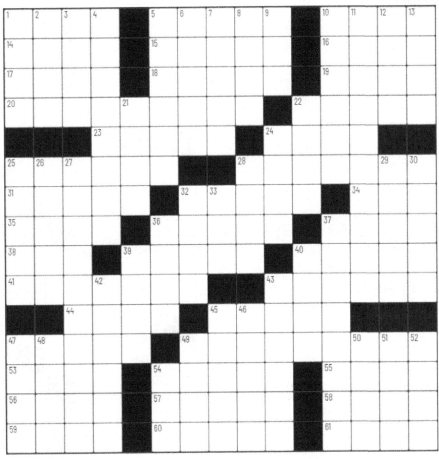

DOWN

1. Open-handed hit
2. Largest of the Three Bears
3. Higher than
4. Most delicious
5. Pictures in an album
6. Arrest, informally
7. Black-and-white cookies
8. __ and groan (complain)
9. NBC weekend sketch show, for short
10. West Texas city
11. Minor enough to excuse
12. Get __ the ground floor
13. "__ la vie!"
21. Puts frosting on
22. Grasped in one's hand
24. Banana covering
25. Mexican snacks in shells
26. Online message
27. Great Britain's legislature
28. Life stories, for short
29. Lip cosmetic
30. Frozen rain
32. Drove too fast
33. Holder of peas
36. Appear to be
37. Story summaries
39. Potato, slangily
40. Bartlett or Bosc
42. Airport arrivals
43. Tries to prevent
45. Gown fabric
46. Made an attempt
47. The latest happenings
48. Garfield's pooch pal
49. Without additives
50. Girl explorer of cartoons
51. Bacterium
52. "So what __ is new?"
54. Long-term bank investments: Abbr.

★☆☆

ACROSS

1. Go beyond on the road
5. Southeast Florida city
10. Apex
14. Very much
15. Playful trick
16. Imperfection
17. Spot of land in the sea
18. Blackened, as a chimney flue
19. Golfer's warning shout
20. Entryway signal
22. Packs of playing cards
23. Christmas carols
24. Anklet or argyle
25. Makes broader
28. Tortilla with toppings
31. Not quite right
32. Like a lot
34. Luau necklace
35. "Winning __ everything"
36. Cross the goal line
37. Use a phone
38. Midmorning hour
39. Army instructor, informally
40. Slice up, as a turkey
41. Germ-free
43. Gave shape to
44. Tenant's payment
45. Occupy the throne
47. After-bath garments
49. Urban vehicle's emergency signal
53. Brother of Cain
54. Roof overhangs
55. Despicable
56. Bottom of a shoe
57. Parcel of land
58. 24-hr. cash sources
59. Grasped in one's hand
60. River mouth
61. Not as expensive

DOWN

1. Settled a bill
2. In addition
3. One-person performance
4. Most strict
5. Pulverizes, as potatoes
6. How fries are fried
7. Molecule parts
8. Tiny amount
9. Frosty
10. Have an influence on
11. Bedroom wake-up signal
12. Grade on an exam
13. Mothers of lambs
21. Pros and __
22. Medicinal amount
24. Feeling achy
25. Stands in line
26. "That'll do it for me"
27. "Supper's ready" signal
28. Ripped up
29. Dig deeply (into)
30. Was feeling poorly
32. Farmland measure
33. Spaniel or setter
36. Pretzel topping
37. Traveling show with rides
39. Transgressions
40. Gear teeth
42. Walked unsteadily
43. Spanish celebration
45. Competitor
46. Build, as a house
47. Poison-ivy reaction
48. Woodwind instrument
49. Cab-ride cost
50. Religious ceremony
51. Shade trees
52. Loch __ monster
54. Approximate takeoff hour: Abbr.

ACROSS

1. Would like to have
5. 24-hr. cash devices
9. In addition
13. Underneath
14. Maple or elm
15. Gather up, as crops
16. Improper, as influence
17. Song
18. Rooster or stallion
19. NHL champs' award
21. Pizzeria appliance
22. Bouquet holder
23. Remove creases in clothes
24. Divides up with others
28. Nautical greeting
30. Des Moines' state
31. Submits a paperless tax return
34. GI support grp.
37. Top military award
40. Sailor's distress signal
41. Lime/gin cocktail
42. Not doing anything
43. Edible ice-cream holder
44. Traditional Arctic dome homes
46. Book of maps
49. Brother of Cain
51. "Grizzly" beast
52. Top county-fair award
58. Poker pot payment
59. Teapot toppers
60. Eagle's claw
61. Tips of shoes
62. Leave out
63. French-style pancake
64. Makes mistakes
65. Crowd's disapproving sounds
66. Cuts down with an ax

DOWN

1. "Jack and Jill ___ up . . ."
2. Alan of "M*A*S*H"
3. Person, place, or thing
4. Number in a dozen
5. Lawyers: Abbr.
6. Temporary peace
7. Restaurant's list
8. Leak slowly
9. Weapons depot
10. Depart
11. Store events
12. Unlocks
13. School-kid vehicle
20. Entered cautiously
23. Very fancy
24. Occupies a chair
25. Sounds from Santa
26. Amazes
27. Lamb's father
28. ___ vera (skin cream ingredient)
29. More weighty
32. Renown
33. Not feeling well
34. Loosen, as laces
35. One-person performance
36. Rocks from a mine
38. Self-images
39. Liquid for frying
43. Affectionate touch
45. Minor malfunction
46. Subside
47. Voice above bass
48. In a little while
49. Sound in a broadcast
50. Personal top scores
52. Drop of paint
53. Chauffeured car, for short
54. Undecorated
55. Inflated, with "up"
56. Clumsy one's remark
57. U-turn from SSW

Puzzle #38

ACROSS

1. Altitudes: Abbr.
5. Remove the rind from
9. Egyptian snakes
13. __ Antoinette (French queen)
14. Utilizes
15. Casual conversation
16. Windowsill cactus, for example
17. "Please reply" invitation letters
18. Make do somehow
19. Breakfast potatoes
21. Tube for sipping a soda
22. Castaway's escape vehicle
23. Industrious insect
24. High __ (elite group)
28. Takes a stand against
32. "Lucky" four-leaf find
33. Buddies
34. Small amt. of sugar
35. Not doing anything
36. Major blood vessel
38. Computer input
39. Provided with a meal
40. Land measure
41. Dish under a teacup
43. Where pet hamsters live
45. Swimming movements
46. Superlative suffix
47. Injure seriously
48. School grades
50. Eye-opening breakfast beverage
55. Triple-decker cookie
56. Tube-shaped pasta
57. Very funny people
58. Boyfriend
59. __ so (nevertheless)
60. Revises a manuscript
61. Seasoning in a shaker
62. Snakelike swimmers
63. Ration (out)

DOWN

1. Angel topper
2. Nutrient measure
3. Fork prong
4. Let loose or release
5. Filter for drinking, as water
6. Selling point
7. Guns, as an engine
8. Sixth sense, for short
9. Credit card ID: Abbr.
10. Small pancake order
11. Largest of the Three Bears
12. Souplike beef dish
13. Speedometer letters
20. Hectic daily routine
21. Drains of energy
24. Spaceship story genre
25. __ days (long ago)
26. Corn flakes or raisin bran
27. "Now __ seen everything!"
28. Grain in Cheerios
29. What credit cards are made of
30. Lauder of cosmetics
31. Practices boxing
33. Opposite of post-
37. Surgeons' workplaces: Abbr.
38. Musical twosome
40. FBI or CIA workers
42. Covered in steel, as a tank
44. Invite on a date
45. Shiny fabrics
47. Lodging near a highway
48. Unruly crowds
49. Vicinity
50. Bee's home
51. Generic dog name
52. Aluminum wrap
53. Suffix with luncheon
54. Superman's insignia
56. Alphabet's end

ACROSS

1. Prefix meaning "one"
5. Here today, __ tomorrow
9. Close friends
13. Donated
14. Puts frosting on
15. Operatic solo
16. Watchful and ready
17. Gusto
18. Gas in store-window signs
19. Wide-angle views
21. Express gratitude to
22. Letters following ems
23. Get __ the ground floor
24. Mrs. in Spain
25. Servings of butter
26. Intimidates
29. Take a breath
32. Successful negotiation
34. Sharp, as intellect
35. Tied, as shoestrings
37. Huron or Superior
38. Survey of people who just voted
40. Considered to be
42. Group of traveling performers
43. Competes in a marathon
44. Mrs. in France
45. Snake's tooth
46. Donkey
49. Piece of bacon
52. People in discussion groups
54. Weaving machine
55. Polio conqueror Jonas
56. Guy who writes jingles
57. Initial poker chip
58. Otherwise
59. Gets close to
60. Hive insects
61. Unwanted lawn plant
62. Father's Day honorees

DOWN

1. Northern Italian city

2. Baking appliances
3. Infamous Roman emperor
4. Facing a jury
5. Gadgets
6. Atlantic or Pacific
7. Loch __ monster
8. Superlative suffix
9. Long, narrow regions of Texas and Florida
10. Vicinity
11. Jungle roarer
12. Plummeted
13. Stare open-mouthed
20. "Where the deer and the __ play"
21. Factual
24. Mound in the Sahara
25. Performs without talking
26. Female deer
27. Sports squad

28. "For Pete's __!"
29. Eisenhower nickname
30. __-door neighbor
31. Legacy recipient
32. 650, in Roman numerals
33. Was in first place
36. Pub beverage
39. Gasoline dispenser
41. London's country
43. Placed in order
45. Not factual
46. Comparable to a wet hen
47. Film's top performers
48. Nine-digit IDs
49. Thick slice
50. Voicemail beep
51. Repetitive learning method
52. Drained of color
53. Notion
55. Work with needle and thread

ACROSS

1. Castaways' escape vehicles
6. "That's funny!"
10. Oil cartel letters
14. Musical work for sopranos
15. List-shortening abbr.
16. Tiresome speaker
17. Tin or aluminum
18. Lounge around
19. Actor Alda
20. Man's throat bulge
22. Boat's pole
23. Mornings: Abbr.
24. Looks angrily (at)
26. Rough, as sandpaper
30. Make an escape
32. "You can leave now"
33. Decide not to visit
35. Dog's tiny pests
40. About to say "Here's to you"
43. Enthusiastic
44. Grassy fields
45. Soft French cheese
46. Full collections
48. Future attorney's field of study
50. Green pasta sauces
54. Lion of the zodiac
55. At any __ (nevertheless)
56. Gambling token
63. Fairy tale meanie
64. Plow-pulling beasts
65. Lamp covering
66. Prepare for, as a vacation
67. Offend the nose
68. Spud
69. Uses needle and thread
70. Clucking sounds of disapproval
71. T-bone or porterhouse

DOWN

1. Italy's capital, to natives
2. Imitated
3. Cheese in Greek salads
4. Airport shuttle vehicle
5. Spicy Mexican dips
6. Assists
7. On the roof of
8. School corridor
9. Claim without proof
10. President from 2009-2017
11. __ bear (Arctic mammal)
12. Remove pencil marks
13. Pennies
21. Make __ of (botch)
25. Went away
26. Deal with adversity
27. Vegetable in gumbo
28. Wildly excited
29. Lasso
30. Speeders' penalties
31. Women's golf org.
34. Bagpiper's garment
36. Tip of the ear
37. __ Grey tea
38. India's continent
39. Slow-cooker meal
41. Approximately
42. Colorado ski resort
47. Accompany to a party
49. Henhouse perches
50. Theater accessories
51. "Bald" bird
52. Scarecrow filling
53. Kids older than 12
54. Parts of a chain necklace
57. Lumberjacks' tools
58. Search for
59. Casual conversation
60. Detest
61. Creative thought
62. Enliven, with "up"

ACROSS

1. Don't get along
6. Ibsen protagonist
10. Triangular sails
14. Topping with pine nuts
15. Biblical role for Crowe
16. Pastel shade
17. Happening shortly
18. "Self" starter
19. Cookout supply
20. Strip mall lessors
23. TGIF part
24. Glitch
25. Easy mark
27. Northwestern legend
31. Predicament
33. Field of expertise
34. Floor decoration
38. Maryland's state bird
42. Metal in lead alloys
43. Roman moon goddess
44. Cobbled together
45. Road-surfacing stuff
48. Very lean one
51. Tennis great on a 2005 stamp
52. Sine __ non
53. Rig product
60. "Trinity" author
62. Oceanic predator
63. Pinterest upload
64. Piedmont wine center
65. Modest poker hand
66. Childish comeback
67. Places at stake
68. Cut corners, say
69. Hangs in there

DOWN

1. Some Navy noncoms
2. Post-Carnival period
3. Concerning
4. Play the lead
5. "Fingers crossed!"
6. Bother persistently
7. Immature
8. "Great" kid-lit sleuth
9. Superhero based on Norse myth
10. Sharp remark
11. "That's it for me"
12. Batters' tactics
13. Insolent
21. Yoko __
22. Wild animal's trail
26. As one pleases
27. Cake with rum
28. Persian Gulf land
29. Moolah
30. Daughter of Mohammed
31. Nautical pronoun
32. Hotshot
34. Test out
35. Defeat decisively
36. Below-elbow bone
37. Camping stuff
39. Mature insect
40. Stylish, during Beatlemania
41. Undivided
45. Key left of D
46. "The plot thickens!"
47. Up in the sky
48. Fledgling pigeon
49. Evil spell
50. Bonnie of blues-rock
51. PC character format
54. Dandy dressers
55. Football great Tarkenton
56. Ryan's "La La Land" costar
57. Horse course
58. " __ Plenty o' Nuttin'"
59. Most with August birthdays
61. Family nickname

ACROSS

1. Gemstone measure
6. Relative of the apple
10. Donkey sound
14. Fill with joy
15. Stone of "La La Land"
16. Display of anger
17. First Greek letter
18. Stated
19. Church affirmation
20. Bad-luck bringer, e.g.
23. Eve's home
24. Remain hidden
25. Finance deg.
28. Tranquil
30. View a film online
32. WWII sub
36. Artist Warhol
37. Alligators in sewers, e.g.
41. Ship of 1492
43. Fencing swords
44. Newspaper bigwig
47. Distinctive periods
52. Two-year-old
53. Works with a loom
57. Small talk
58. Toads cause warts, e.g.
60. Elongated pasta
63. Hamster's home
64. Canned tomato product
65. Clickable image
66. ___ to (just like)
67. "Come in!"
68. Sneak a look
69. Hit with snowballs
70. Gardener's bane

DOWN

1. Discontinues
2. Make reference (to)
3. Struck, as a door
4. Wise Greek goddess
5. Pull apart
6. Green sauce
7. Internet messages
8. Ever so slightly
9. Half a diameter
10. Grain husk
11. Sheep with horns
12. Distinctive period
13. Strong desire
21. Queen of ___ (Old Testament figure)
22. Pick, with "for"
25. Repair
26. Behaving poorly
27. Poehler of "Parks and Recreation"
29. Butter container
31. Scooted away
33. Small bill
34. Austrian peak
35. Golf peg
37. Subsidiary company
38. Double-crosser
39. V-shaped fliers
40. Sixth sense, for short
41. After-tax amount
42. Bachelor's last words
45. Night bird
46. Baggage handler
48. Stat on gas pumps
49. Totally virtuous
50. Stopped marching
51. Controls the wheel
54. Fully conscious
55. Continuous watch
56. Social gathering
58. Sty sound
59. Gush forth
60. Read quickly, with "through"
61. Polar formation
62. Tip of a sock

ACROSS

1. Family nickname
5. 1981 Oscar winner as Loretta
10. Holds up
14. Colossal
15. Show regret
16. Crunchy cheesecake ingredient
17. Emma Bovary creator
20. Mall tenant, often
21. Stable sound
22. Disparaging remark
24. Profs' helpers
25. Links org.
27. DOJ arm
28. Whodunit elements
30. Hassle, for short
31. Little tree climber
32. Parisian prayer addressee
33. Fancy trimmings
35. "Show Boat" impresario
39. Word on the South American capitals list
40. Has a balance
43. Crock, for one
46. Capture by surprise
47. Not inert
49. Hosp. area
50. Facebook giggle
51. Swampy spot
52. Squelch
53. Sunlit lobbies
55. Rotten
57. Adapts easily
62. Olympics implement
63. Strike down, old-style
64. Evening in Pisa
65. Pitchfork prong
66. Distance runner
67. Poetic tributes

DOWN

1. Eldest of the "Little Women"
2. "The Simpsons" shopkeeper
3. Troublemaker's doings
4. Overture follower
5. File-menu command
6. News bits
7. Sectional, e.g.
8. NBC skit show
9. Assenting vote
10. Boxer's garb
11. Big potato processor
12. Norwegian port
13. With the result being
18. Social starter
19. Without the wherewithal
22. Terrible
23. Will Smith biopic role
25. Very fussy ones
26. Part of 25 Across
29. Eyedropper part
30. Hospital area
33. Ultimate
34. Problematic roommate
36. Western stock character
37. Not a one
38. Declined gradually
41. Manning in a huddle
42. Gender
43. Rolex alternative
44. Squid cousins
45. Serving piece
47. Nature personified
48. Fairy tale giant
51. Vertical-sided hill
54. "Got it!"
55. Punxsutawney groundhog
56. "In that case ..."
58. Doctrine
59. "We don't need to hear that"
60. Underground resource
61. Took place

Puzzle #44

ACROSS

1. Church chimers
6. Mouse-catching device
10. One-for-one trade
14. Annoyed greatly
15. Cash in France
16. Hydrant attachment
17. Oreo filling
18. Minor error
19. __ and crafts
20. Chamomile beverages
22. Short parody
23. Spring month
24. Source of fries, slangily
26. Rode the rapids, perhaps
30. Video game self-image
32. Pungent-smelling
33. Snowman's neck covering
34. Bikini top
37. Boutique
38. Mends, as socks
39. Split apart
40. Dispenser candy
41. Flood blocker
42. Fragment
43. Makes joyful
45. Northernmost state
46. Take charge of
48. Restful resort
49. Snakes like Cleo's
50. Rough sailing conditions
57. "Don't delete" mark
58. Package-sealing roll
59. Telecast's sound
60. Word-of-mouth
61. Israeli airline
62. Statement of faith
63. Too curious
64. Farmer's spot of song
65. Fundamental belief

DOWN

1. Composer Johann Sebastian
2. Raison d'__
3. Impolite look
4. Woolly infant
5. Cooked over boiling water
6. Short-tempered
7. Regulation
8. Diva's solo
9. Musical celebrities
10. Northern California peak
11. Most hive females
12. Up and about
13. Annoyances
21. Young fellow
25. Anti-moonshine org.
26. Speak hoarsely
27. Need a massage
28. They're thawed for dinner
29. Bit of useful advice
30. Much land
31. Barn-top instrument
33. Goalie's success
35. Holder of spices
36. District
38. Got wind of
39. Spanish aunt
41. Fall behind
42. Perform a role on stage
44. "In conclusion . . ."
45. Software download
46. Brick worker
47. Houston athlete
48. Wizard's casting
51. __ and hearty
52. Cameo stone
53. "Of course!"
54. Genesis setting
55. Right-hand person
56. Chimney buildup

ACROSS

1. Talk defiantly
5. Toddler's cupful
9. Etcher's purchase
14. Make a stocking cap
15. Resting upon
16. Sonata movement
17. "Beats me"
20. Free from excitement
21. Certain credit-card accepter
22. Trees of the mimosa family
25. Literary fantasy land
29. Community service group
30. In a blaze
32. Socially awkward one
33. Disciple of Socrates
34. Of charged 6 Down
36. Astaire-era studio
37. "Beats me"
40. Barnyard beast
42. Products of the imagination
43. Did a blacksmith's job
46. Tear apart
48. ISP selection
49. Stretches in the service
50. Cash in
52. Get in touch with
53. Roth plans
55. Busy as __
56. "Beats me"
63. Lightens up
64. Outranking
65. "Got it"
66. Livelihood
67. Inn furniture
68. French state

DOWN

1. Glide down Alps
2. Colony member
3. Family nickname
4. Choppy, to Chopin
5. Accost unexpectedly
6. Elemental material
7. Was elected
8. Jungle beasts
9. Specialized vocabulary
10. Discount ticket
11. Suffix for salt
12. Periodontist's designation
13. Signal for help
18. Frequent safari starting point
19. Place under quarantine
22. Abstract artist Jean or Hans
23. Maj.'s superior
24. Done with
26. Outward image
27. Exasperate
28. Fuss
30. True to one's cause
31. Alternatives to toner
34. Mid-March day
35. 2012 Emmy winner as a Hatfield
38. Guy said to be "out"
39. Formal attire
40. Bungle up
41. Totlike
44. Shortened series ender
45. Mar.-Nov. period
47. Cleaned for a frosty takeoff
49. Quits joking around
51. Make a clean slate
52. Fell to persuasion
54. Smug expert
56. Thus far
57. Blade for some boats
58. Basic cable channel
59. The night before Christmas
60. Indicator of ultimateness
61. Grazing land
62. Give the go-ahead to

ACROSS

1. Tire-surface pattern
6. Loads a suitcase
11. Top poker card
14. Jim of the Alamo
15. Unaccompanied
16. Early evening hour
17. Classroom competition
19. __ Lanka
20. Convince
21. Consequence
23. Brainy
25. Minimal amounts
26. Italian resort isle
30. Furious
32. Boise's state
33. Postal delivery
34. Chimp or orangutan
37. With 39 Across, Canadian baseballer
39. See 37 Across
42. NH winter hours
43. Margin
45. Butcher shop device
46. Less strict
48. University housing
49. Great bargain
52. State-run game
55. Outspoken
57. Capacities of autos
62. Choose, with "for"
63. Slugger's club
65. "__ the ramparts . . ."
66. Speech opener
67. British singer of "Skyfall"
68. Be a snoop
69. Final authority
70. Ignited again

DOWN

1. Cookbook amt.
2. Lariat
3. Water pitcher
4. Feels unwell
5. False belief
6. Bear native to China
7. North African nation
8. Corn's core
9. Bendable leg part
10. Consider it suitable
11. Strong point
12. About the year of
13. Leaves a building
18. "__ so sorry!"
22. Adversary
24. Large family
26. Make mention of
27. Commotions
28. Acting role
29. Letter after pi
31. Everyone
33. Fashion show poser
34. Slightly open
35. Coconut tree
36. Hurricane centers
38. __-Mex cuisine
40. Amer. money
41. "Green" prefix
44. Food merchants
46. Young boy
47. Courtroom explanations
49. Ice cream serving
50. Come to a point
51. Contest submission
53. Not allowed
54. __ la la
56. Comic Carvey
58. Merrie __ England
59. Eve's second son
60. Artist Salvador
61. Proofreader's mark
64. Structure for swine

ACROSS

1. Untrustworthy one
4. Blondie's hubby
7. Dog show org.
10. Meadow grazer
13. Brink
14. Make a misstep
15. Argentine "one"
16. "Caught you!"
17. Stamping device
18. Southwest English city
20. Respectful title
21. Mouse hunter
22. Thorough, as a cleaning
24. Thoroughly
26. Itsy-bitsy
27. Country-style
28. Wind-farm parts
30. Respectful title
33. Thin
34. Liquid-Plumr rival
35. Prolonged look
37. How English is read
41. In the wind
42. Unwitting victims
45. New Jersey senator Booker
49. Go (for)
50. Be ambitious
51. Fields of expertise
53. East ender
55. Thin
56. In reverse, in a way
60. ___-Wan Kenobi
61. Corroded
62. Superhero group member
63. Winning streak
64. Show that you understand
65. Intersected
66. OPEC member
67. Frat letter
68. Add up to
69. Historic starter
70. Certain lodge member
71. Oscar actor Benicio __ Toro

DOWN

1. Diamond or heart
2. Either Wright brother
3. Shun spirits
4. Fiscal issue
5. Hamlet's slings partner
6. Moan and groan
7. Shutter speed setting
8. Dresser grip
9. Anecdotal commentary
10. '50s revolutionary
11. Either Wright brother
12. With cordiality
19. Thoroughly, at sea
23. Rhyme trio's vessel
25. Neighborhood designation
29. Internet guffaw
31. Almost never found
32. Word on the Asian nation list
35. Knock it off
36. Batter ingredients
38. Unduly
39. Brewery basics
40. Made to order
43. Elaborate recognition
44. Highly original
45. Beach club amenity
46. Eloquent one
47. Move away
48. Talk without a break
50. Temper, as titanium
52. Imprint
54. Untrustworthy one
57. Exceeding
58. Gala event
59. Hardly a walk in the park

Puzzle #48

ACROSS

1. Be an omen of
5. Sharp knocks
9. Support, as with a wager
14. Numbered musical work
15. Polish a manuscript
16. Make amends
17. Submit one's ballot
19. Sample of food
20. Acid neutralizer
21. Diplomatic skill
23. Lawn material
24. Narrate
26. Island nation near Sicily
28. Concerning this, in legalese
30. Motive
33. Chimp, for one
35. Scouting group
37. Garden digging tool
38. Woodpecker's nose
40. Buddy
41. Apply the brakes
42. Underground chambers
44. High-fives, for example
47. Gallery display
48. Catches some Z's
50. Uttered
52. Into pieces
54. Messes up
55. "60 Minutes" network
57. Games with no winner
59. The 1990s, for instance
63. Celebrity roster
65. Display anger
67. Scoundrel
68. Parade spoiler
69. Urge on
70. Erstwhile anesthetic
71. Finds a sum
72. Innumerable years

DOWN

1. __ Raton, FL
2. Whitish gem
3. Twilight
4. Many-acre residence
5. One expressing contempt
6. Fuss
7. Actor Brad
8. Radiator output
9. Military engagements
10. Greek vowel
11. Prepare lunch, perhaps
12. Not fooled by
13. Must have
18. Fully awake
22. Hyundai or Honda
25. Stunt flying maneuvers
27. Touches on the shoulder
28. Express relief
29. Young horses
31. Scent
32. Small salamander
33. Reading basics
34. Church-bell sound
36. Dinner holder
39. Don't throw out
43. Produce stray drops
45. Forgives
46. Scatter around
49. __ Lanka
51. Avoid capture
53. Aquarium fish
55. Feel concern
56. Ink stain
58. Type of herring
60. Spherical hairdo
61. Singer Celine
62. Approximate takeoff hrs.
64. Novelist Grafton
66. Get __ of (throw out)

ACROSS

1. Up-and-down signals
5. Pokémon video genre
10. Folklore brute
14. "Rigoletto" solo
15. "Do right" lesson
16. Offering to a judge
17. Many a Civil War image
19. Even-number Interstate heading
20. Supermodel Crawford
21. Some cutter crew
23. Sports-drink brand suffix
24. That "femme"
26. Hosiery thread
29. "Phooey!"
31. Sweet bread spread
34. "Big Blue" business
36. Elitist
37. Biceps location
38. "No fooling?"
42. What a pointer might say
44. Venerable news source
45. Doodled
47. Barcelona bravo
48. Place for odds and ends
51. Play makeup
55. Bit of a subscription
56. Liking a lot
58. On like a lantern
59. Native (to)
62. Safe IRA investment
64. Pirate's beverage
66. A Maritime province
68. Irk
69. Psi follower
70. Hoax
71. Essence of vegan "meatballs"
72. Fully filled
73. Some lady birds

DOWN

1. Speedway acronym
2. Big potato processor
3. Aquarium scooper
4. Spoken
5. Band's blaster
6. Useless
7. Laundry staff
8. Padded play surfaces
9. Wells' idle race
10. Gift giver's encouragement
11. Boxer's vulnerability
12. Hi-__ graphics
13. Cook's encouragement
18. Matey's assent
22. Planet-wide
25. Hedy of Hollywood
27. Zhivago's love
28. Honor for a sitcom
30. Knightly title
32. Bank acct. accrual
33. Accomplice
35. Went to sleep, with "down"
38. Japan's highest peak
39. Composer's numbered piece
40. Remove suds from
41. Grazing expanse
43. It may be in the bag
46. GI Bill beneficiary
49. Self-defense skill
50. Confine, as a canary
52. Give garb to
53. Italian Renaissance artist
54. Cooks, as dim sum
57. Non-prescription, for short
60. Son of Seth
61. NY home of Chagalls
63. Quick bite
64. BBC clock setting
65. Site of the 2016 Olympics
67. Unfortunate

Puzzle #50

ACROSS

1. Canine comment
5. Train for a bout
9. No more than
13. Jai __
14. __ Antoinette (French queen)
15. Adolescent
16. "Just tell me when"
18. With 32 Down, color like turquoise
19. Texter's "As I see it"
20. Metallic rocks
21. Sundae garnish
23. Providing good traction
25. Blacken on the grill
26. Kitty or canary
27. Novels' high points
31. Monks' home
34. As compared to
35. Plane flight assignment
36. Courtroom statement
37. Serious play
38. Predatory dolphin
39. Vast majority
40. Sound hoarse
41. Thick, as eyebrows
42. Successful on one's own
44. Make illegal
45. Throw a tantrum
46. Ship maintenance area
50. Twitter messages
53. Italian farewell
54. Hunters' org.
55. Center of a bagel
56. Get down to business
59. Squashed circle
60. Fencing swords
61. Floor model
62. Depend (on)
63. Football officials, briefly
64. Affirmative votes

DOWN

1. Boats' mooring place
2. San Antonio shrine
3. Synthetic fabric
4. Something to assemble
5. Made two-by-fours
6. Country club instructors
7. Ventilate
8. Mao's realm
9. Break the silence
10. Look keenly
11. Rip (up)
12. Nothing but
14. Be worthy of
17. Corny
22. Meat in an omelet
24. Utter what's on your mind
25. Vise, for example
27. Pursue
28. Gen-___ (boomers' kids)
29. Individually
30. Hang around
31. Police dept. alerts
32. See 18 Across
33. Elementary school signal
34. Swap
37. Racing vehicle
41. Louisiana wetland
43. Doorstep covering
44. Unruly children
46. Flood blockers
47. Tonally accurate
48. Sandwich cookie filling
49. Bout enders
50. Norse thunder god
51. Made, as a tapestry
52. Israeli airline
53. Symbol starting a line of music
57. Chimp or orangutan
58. Vitamin dose standard: Abbr.

Puzzle #51

ACROSS

1. "Faithful" Seuss character
7. Apple computer
11. School lunch standby, briefly
14. Olay competitor
15. 11 Wall St. tenant
16. Boom-box button
17. Memorable indecisive Dane
18. Boom-box component
20. Bottom-line PC key
21. It touches Thailand
22. Tapered shape
23. UK mega-author
26. Mouselike mammal
27. Plane controller
28. It's over your head
29. Interrogative "And how!"
30. Stop for the "Bounty"
33. Lunch order from Mom
36. Wool source
37. They're scanned in e-commerce
38. Sports figure
39. Family nickname
40. Bottle of sample perfume
41. "Am __ understand . . ."
42. Start of Grafton's eighth "Alphabet" title
43. "Friends" star
46. Show sudden interest
49. Body art that fluoresces
51. __ chatter (gossip mag fodder?)
52. Two-person Olympic event
53. Workout venue
54. Geometry coordinate systems
56. Literary likening
59. Half-rectangle shapes
60. Indirect assistance
61. Ribbons and medals
62. Slick or quick with tricks
63. Throws in
64. Naval assemblages

DOWN

1. Shout of defiance
2. Latin eggs
3. Took a second?
4. Describe
5. Combo punch
6. "__ bad!"
7. Alpaca breeder of old
8. Pet owner's Pinterest post header
9. African snakes
10. Art in animation books
11. Richard of stand-up
12. Geoffrey of fashion
13. L.L. Bean alternative
19. Feeling sore
21. Purple flowers
23. Bored by it all
24. Oklahoma tribe
25. Petrol measures
26. Glides on snow
28. Chest bones
31. Sultry
32. Put some thought to
33. Paint a perfect picture of
34. Threepio's pal
35. Art in animation books
37. Cotton stick brand
42. Pea pod, essentially
44. Socialite celebrity
45. Thwart
46. Low poker pair
47. Pastoral poem
48. __-turvy
49. Flip over
50. Snug men's wear
52. City in Oklahoma
55. "I see the light!"
56. Sunscreen stat.
57. Ending like -ette
58. Double curve

Puzzle #52

ACROSS

1. Wish earnestly
5. Golf pegs
9. Conclude logically
14. Wicked
15. Folklore fiend
16. Nick of films
17. Monopoly train line
20. Very stubborn
21. Weed-removing tool
22. Basketball tie-breakers: Abbr.
23. New parents' lawn ornament
24. Farmer, in springtime
27. Stores away
28. Apple computer
30. Most expensive Monopoly property
35. New Delhi garments
37. Comics explosion sound
38. Special skill
39. No longer edible
40. Second most expensive Monopoly property
43. City in Mo.
44. Backyard barbecue area
45. Eluded capture
47. In different places
52. Lamb's father
54. Show on television
55. Stock exchange worker
56. Monopoly utility
60. Gift recipient
61. Sharp, as eyesight
62. Friends of Tarzan
63. Aquatic mammal
64. Natural balm
65. Proofreader's notation

DOWN

1. Tubular sandwiches
2. In plain sight
3. Cocktail lounge instrument

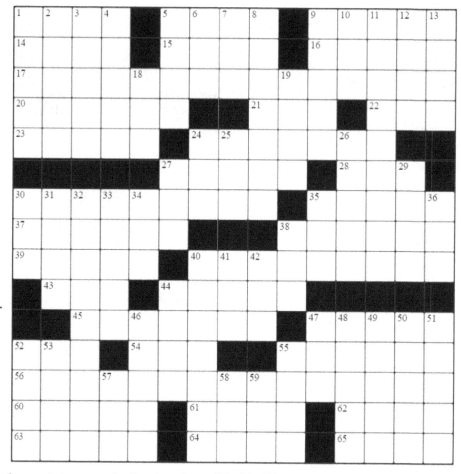

4. __ statesman (retired male politician)
5. Broadway prize
6. Soufflé ingredient
7. Make a blunder
8. Fish-eating bird
9. Small bay
10. Likewise not
11. Carpeting measurement
12. Coup d'__
13. Wine category
18. Annoy
19. Charged atoms
24. After-school org.
25. Texter's "That's funny!"
26. Place to cyber-shop
27. Personal ad abbr.
29. Presidential title: Abbr.
30. Library vols.
31. Granola morsels
32. Reduction, as in tax

33. Diner basketful
34. Fawn's mother
35. Deprive of strength
36. Canonized Fr. woman
38. Fight stoppage, for short
40. Goulash seasoning
41. Wolfed down
42. Get __ of (discard)
44. Twosome
46. Do a banquet job
47. Escort's offering
48. Family men, informally
49. Modify to fit
50. Actress Zellweger
51. Secret meeting
52. Make over
53. Very many
55. Voice quality
57. Middling grade
58. Plastic animation sheet
59. Boardroom VIP

ACROSS

1. __-pedal (play down)
5. May honorees
10. Hubbub
14. "Inter __" (among others)
15. Not as expected
16. Out of town
17. Heinz varieties
19. Prefix for phone
20. Prior night
21. Weather-changing current
22. Cognizant of
23. Flipper's transaction
25. Be over by
27. Arrive by air
30. Compliments to the chef
33. Western uplands
36. Terse denial
38. Columbus sch.
39. Qatari leader
40. Tiny bits
41. Knit-fabric flaw
42. Blender output
43. Single
44. Industrious ones
45. Frisky swimmers
47. Address of colonial India
49. Matriculated New Havenite
51. Maine national park
55. Sound of disappearance
57. Not at all erratic
60. Stress test display
61. Organic soother
62. Signers of the U.S. Constitution
64. Decant
65. Chill-inducing
66. Cultural figure
67. Somewhat off
68. Utility room machine
69. Little lizard

DOWN

1. Not as hazardous
2. Yellowish green
3. Piccolo cousins
4. Art on an arm
5. Walter of crime fiction
6. Yemeni port
7. Early 16th-century date
8. Coeur d'__, ID
9. Mean and nasty
10. Seuss' eggs-and-ham offerer
11. Spots on a die
12. "Othello" antagonist
13. TV host Seacrest
18. Outcries
24. Miles off
26. Expected in
28. "__ pronounce you . . ."
29. Written reminders
31. On call military org.
32. Coffee carriers
33. Written reminder
34. Send forth
35. Squares on a checkerboard
37. "And here it is!"
40. Wouldn't bend
41. Japanese noodles
43. Web ID
44. Rather risky
46. Diner, for one
48. Summer top
50. Old anesthetic
52. Scrape, as a windshield
53. "Not news here"
54. Contract negotiator
55. June honoree
56. Proceed smoothly
58. Open to breezes
59. Cheese in a wheel
63. French diarist

Puzzle #54

ACROSS

1. Thaws
6. Barton of the Red Cross
11. Chemist's workplace
14. Author/poet T.S.
15. Petroleum-carrying vessel
16. Rock that's mined
17. Acidity-testing strip
19. Letters on Postal Service stamps
20. Fawn or doe
21. One of the Beatles
23. Batters' toppers
27. Aquarius and Aries
28. Veggies in omelets
29. Understated
32. Ward off
33. Shows concern
34. Revolutionary Guevara
37. Was a passenger
38. Short pleasure trip
39. "Beg pardon . . ."
40. Tint changer
41. Outdoes
42. Alternative strategy
43. Acquire molars, say
45. Catch sight of
46. Sneaker pattern
48. Applied 40 Across to
49. Disqualify, as a juror
51. Mariner's greeting
52. Appear in a film
53. 38 Down's wheels
59. Small folk singing group
60. "Easy as pie!"
61. Warning signs
62. Go astray
63. Abounds
64. Pester persistently

DOWN

1. Actor Gibson
2. Yale student
3. Ignited
4. Hanks or Cruise
5. Pupil
6. Handles adversity
7. Untruthful one
8. Swiss peak
9. Fishing line holder
10. Takes into custody
11. Piece of patio furniture
12. Fire-setting crime
13. Burrito ingredients
18. Prepares, as an alarm clock
22. Zilch
23. Hidden supply
24. Diplomat
25. Interrogation device
26. Extra amount
29. Fry lightly
30. Large coffee dispensers
31. Casino transaction
33. Dollars and cents
35. From now on
36. Plant firmly
38. Part of an airline fleet
39. Operatic voice
41. Mattress support
42. Triangle or square
44. ___ de Cologne
45. Busy time at urban food trucks
46. Line of work
47. Happen again
48. Crunchy snacks
50. Worry-free feeling
51. Genesis exile
54. Compass pt.
55. A.M. show on ABC
56. Brain wave test: Abbr.
57. Santa ___, Calif.
58. String after Q

Puzzle #55

ACROSS

1. Last word of "The Wizard of Oz"
5. Sounds of laughter
9. Email sent by bots
13. Cameo shape
14. Big name at Tesla
15. Smarter now, perhaps
17. Animal org. with a bunny logo
18. Evocator of laughter
19. Tureen accessory
20. Papers and mags
23. Very vivid, as crayon colors
24. Wall bracket shape
25. Number-picking game
26. "Platinum" shade
28. Transmits, as some messages
30. High-pitched instrument
32. Unkind comment
33. Mud bath venues
34. Avoid embarrassment
36. Little guys
40. Actress Hatcher
41. Begin litigation
45. Ballet move
49. Brewpub designation
50. Give up rights to
51. Obligate
53. Plenty of nothing
55. Castro of Cuba
57. CPA suggestion, maybe
58. Enthusiastic about
59. Unrestricted period
62. French land
64. Temperamental mood
65. Anatomical projection
66. Rolex rival
67. Pinnacle
68. Work with a word processor
69. Taiwanese PC maker
70. Oracle
71. Informal instants

DOWN

1. Lottery ball holders
2. Have coverage in common
3. Title girl of a Dahl novel
4. Special flair
5. Mercury alias
6. Any "Star Wars" person
7. Jinxes
8. Prefix for oxidant
9. Scale note
10. Dallas suburb
11. Supplementary material
12. Singable
16. Go back (on)
21. Fight stopper of a sort
22. Superior to
27. Sidelong look
29. Ireland or Iceland
31. Mammalian pollinator
35. Bubble's exterior
37. "The Nazarene" author
38. Resulting from
39. "Science Kid" toon
41. "Done!"
42. Rio beach
43. Half an artist's surname
44. Roman comic playwright
46. About 22 current-sitcom minutes
47. Workout category
48. Astrological influences
51. Civil War's "Boy General"
52. Jai alai shout
54. Small canyon
56. Japanese cartoons
60. Smokey Bear TV spots
61. Beverages labeled 49 Across
63. 65 Across locale

ACROSS

1. __ Lee cakes
5. Minor error
9. Swap
14. Shape of a face
15. Deep sleep
16. Inflexible
17. Give up, as territory
18. Stadium crowd sound
19. Insurance broker
20. British bat-and-ball competition
23. Double-curve
24. Woolly female
25. Of food programs
29. Back-to-health program, for short
31. Drizzles or showers
33. Compete
34. Apple desktop computer
36. Flavor enhancer initials
37. Police officers, informally
38. Star-Kist competitor
42. Money in Mexico
43. Neighbor of Tarzan
44. Knight's title
45. Brewery product
46. 24 sheets of paper
48. Take home a shelter animal
52. "The Blue Danube" composer
54. Cold-cream container
56. Neither here __ there
57. Inept soldier of the comics
60. Secret stockpile
63. Frilly, as some wedding gowns
64. Petty complaints
65. "French" soup ingredient
66. CPR experts
67. Assemble, as a sweater
68. Top-billed performers
69. Backtalk
70. Parts of a min.

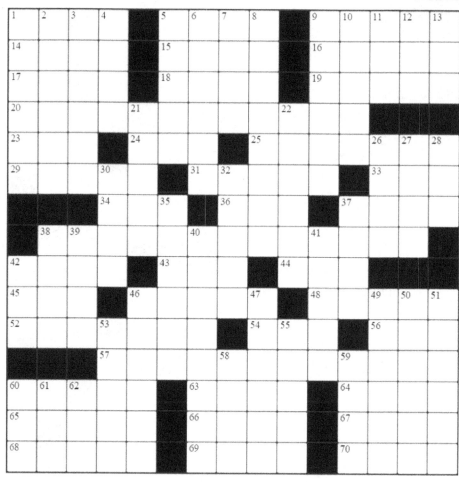

DOWN

1. World Cup sport
2. Reluctant
3. Pungent salad veggie
4. Actor Baldwin
5. Wood fastener
6. Thief during a power outage
7. Mosque leader
8. Blissful place
9. Tracks down
10. "That's correct!"
11. Era
12. Loud noise
13. Summer hrs. in Pittsburgh
21. Meat grilled on a skewer
22. Slight hints of color
26. River near Shakespeare's home
27. Morning TV host Kelly
28. "I agree!"
30. Bullets, for short

32. Traffic light color
35. Contract section
37. Bit of Miss Muffet's meal
38. Suspenders alternative
39. Software purchaser
40. New Testament letters
41. Headgear for a princess
42. Faux __ (minor error)
46. Powerful chess pieces
47. Pops out, as a DVD
49. Connected to the Internet
50. Written in verse
51. Secret meetings
53. Detest
55. Bottomless pit
58. The Dalai __
59. Printers' supplies
60. Businesses: Abbr.
61. Bug in a colony
62. Espionage org.

ACROSS

1. Criticize, so to speak
4. Monomaniacal mariner of fiction
8. Span supporters
14. Go wrong
15. Formal denial
16. "Star Trek" director J.J.
17. Too __ to __
19. Playful knuckle rub
20. Evolve, as events
21. Opera house exclamation
23. Half of a "game" pair
24. Too __ to __
28. Where some MDs work
29. Smart TV brand
31. Industrious ones
32. Gets it
34. Certain drive-thru convenience
36. Ankara cash
37. Too __ to __
41. One with billing issues, perhaps
44. Witty bit
45. Ride with the air
49. Collected abundantly
52. Important physics equation
54. Part of TNT
55. Too __ to __
57. City near Düsseldorf
59. Fuming
60. Very generous gratuities
61. Whole Foods buyer (2017)
64. Too __ to __
66. Group cry for help
67. Very dark
68. Hyundai rival
69. As quickly as possible
70. Casual wear
71. Corn holder

DOWN

1. Gets back to work
2. Smelter stuff
3. Extravagant
4. Part of a Bullwinkle costume
5. Ready for planting, perhaps
6. Busiest airport in the southern US
7. "The Hobbit" hero
8. Banquet nibble
9. First and foremost
10. Panorama
11. Video streaming delay
12. Early Beatles record label
13. GPS reading
18. Stats, for short
22. Plunder
24. Place to hike
25. According to
26. Feast-famine connector
27. Letter closers, briefly
30. Half of a "game" pair
33. Zappos stats
35. GPS display
38. Get dinner delivered
39. No longer in effect
40. "CSI" specimen
41. Pendulum path
42. State school, for short
43. Ring physician's decision
46. On the line
47. Flower in herbal shampoo
48. Old West symbol
50. Boaster's assurance
51. Major leaguer with a "W" cap
53. Drive-thru operator
56. On the level
58. Sonoran sun
60. Sprite sister brand
61. Shakesperean slitherer
62. Scratch up
63. GPS display
65. Unspecified individual

Puzzle #58

ACROSS

1. __ Raton, FL
5. Straight from the garden
10. Drove too fast
14. Iridescent gem
15. Juliet's love
16. Canine visitor to Oz
17. "Tonight Show" host before Fallon
18. Bother incessantly
19. Curved doorway
20. Tailor's measurement
23. Summer shoe
24. Director Spike or Ang
25. Strong drain cleaner
27. Performed
28. Bikini part
31. Fields of expertise
35. Leave in a hurry
37. Bovine bellows
38. Just barely
41. Dealership displays
42. Boxing match
43. Overly demanding
44. Long-running NBC weekend show
45. Pigsty
46. Bro or sis
48. __ for the course (normal)
49. Subtly suggests
54. Learned thoroughly
59. Wood strip
60. Justice Samuel
61. "Sound off" remote button
62. Small clue
63. More cordial
64. Stiffly formal
65. Unable to sit still
66. Summons from a teacher
67. In years past

DOWN

1. Door fasteners
2. Gig for a soprano
3. Religious doctrine
4. So all can hear
5. Without hindrance
6. Crowd sound
7. CPR experts
8. Aquatic mammal with whiskers
9. Innkeeper
10. Performer's platform
11. Place to dock
12. Engrave deeply
13. Homer Simpson shout
21. Tex-Mex dip
22. Homer Simpson neighbor
26. Zac of "High School Musical"
27. What IOUs represent
28. Physiques, informally
29. Goes bad
30. Very pale
31. Fundamentals
32. TV host Seacrest
33. British nobleman
34. Expresses relief
36. Baton Rouge sch.
37. Onetime Chinese chairman
39. Spaniards, for example
40. Flowed back
45. Knee protector
47. Pretend not to hear
48. Pane sealant
50. Musical pace
51. Reject with scorn
52. Storage spot
53. Main subject
54. Rode (down), as a banister
55. Zesty flavor
56. Writer Wiesel
57. Board-game cubes
58. Agenda entry
59. "Steady as __ goes!"

ACROSS

1. Bridges in films
5. Acted out without words
10. Tapers off
14. Henry Ford contemporary
15. Clamorous, as a crowd
16. Front of a ship
17. Send forth
18. Jazz genre
19. South Asian garment
20. Wrangler's accessories
23. Pope during WWII
24. Charitable ones
25. Pompous one
28. Swim meet outfits
31. Spare expenses
33. Solemn assurance
34. Cuban sandwich ingredient
38. CinemaScope production
42. Shangri-la
43. Have control of
44. Major olive oil producer
45. IDs of a sort
48. Arles article
49. Groundhog Day concern
53. Bygone bird
55. Volume with a jacket
59. The rain in Spain
60. All-important
61. Most of 2017's pennies
64. Deep red
65. Bring joy to
66. Island near Corsica
67. Paella veggies
68. Trip odometer button
69. Luminary

DOWN

1. "Average" guy
2. Street often near Maple
3. Bank acct. backer
4. Aperture setting
5. Fusion of miscellany
6. Poker declaration
7. Ingot shaper
8. Become less burdensome
9. Antonym of 65 Across
10. Seiko's printer brand
11. Encouraging word
12. Cornfield pest
13. Sandwich staple
21. Thin streaks
22. Acapulco article
25. " . . . even __ speak"
26. Losing streak
27. Debate position
29. Recreational calendar entry
30. Female rabbit
32. Blokes
34. Home for a houseplant
35. Running track, e.g.
36. Miff
37. Critical elements
39. Boast rudely about
40. It may be under the sofa
41. Botch
45. Bugs Bunny address
46. Mag rep's quote
47. Piece of stemware
49. Pointed, as a comment
50. The __, Netherlands
51. Possession of the Netherlands
52. Decisive times
54. Exudes
56. Very unpleasant
57. Flight data
58. Symbol of Scotland
62. League often seen on ESPN
63. Big "Price is Right" prize

Puzzle #60

ACROSS

1. Raindrop sound
5. Blacken in a broiler
9. Dish for a dinner
14. Four-star review
15. Very hard to find
16. Desert spot with water
17. At any time
18. Barge __ (disturb)
19. __ Peak, CO
20. Pay-at-curbside machines
23. Droop, as a mattress
24. On vacation
25. Actress Thurman
28. Kitty's cry
30. Courtroom break
35. Legendary jazz trumpeter
39. Marathon, for one
40. Drained of color
41. Relatives
42. Fairy tale monster
43. List-shortening abbr.
44. Unseen character flaw
47. Place for a pedicure
49. Sharer's pronoun
50. Air quality org.
51. High in calories
54. Touch on the shoulder
56. Trains' storage facilities
62. Big name in ketchup
64. Red Muppet
65. "That's what I'm talkin' about!"
66. Overplay during a play
67. Floor sample
68. Eatery's list
69. Turns off, as a TV's sound
70. Fragrance
71. Biblical paradise

DOWN

1. Get ready, for short
2. Volcanic flow
3. Above
4. Fringe benefits
5. Recoiled in fright
6. Put up, as artwork
7. Fragrance
8. Extend a subscription
9. Sailor of cartoons
10. Dragon's retreat
11. Requests
12. Suit accessory
13. Curvy letter
21. Purina competitor
22. Repairs, as a road
25. Called balls and strikes
26. Sporty Mazda model
27. Lessen, as fears
29. Start the day
31. Gator relative
32. National bird
33. Metal to be recycled
34. "I'm outta here!"
36. Slithery swimmers
37. Compete
38. A big fan of
44. Be unsuccessful
45. Suitable for the lawn or patio
46. Start to unravel
48. Raffle offerings
52. Statement of belief
53. __ up (in hiding)
55. Creditor's demand
56. Barrel of laughs
57. Poker ritual
58. Arsenal supply
59. Oboe insert
60. Copenhagen native
61. Steer clear of
62. Garment border
63. Australian bird

Puzzle #61

ACROSS

1. Other name for Mars
5. Igneous rocks, once
10. Part of Cajun stews
14. Printed words
15. Brainy introvert
16. Nine, on the Seine
17. "Masking" stuff
18. Wingding
19. Canvas structure
20. "Seagoing" December song
23. Director Howard
24. Strange
25. Book of Judges strongman
27. Wound down
29. Hang down
32. Throw with might
33. Tiny bit
35. Tavern container
37. Tavern container
38. "No crib" December song
43. Certain nest egg
44. Dispenser sweet
45. Diner dessert
46. Brief instant
49. Metaphor for deceit
51. Heavy gas
55. With the upshot being
57. Guitar cousin
59. Feminine "a" in French
60. "Merry and bright" December song
64. Signed off on
65. Horse to ride
66. Be at the edge of
67. Used to be
68. Name on western Washington maps
69. Wingding
70. Checked out
71. Paper's essays
72. Stomped (on)

DOWN

1. Raiment
2. Common sense
3. Add more stores
4. Hodgepodge
5. Certain physician's combo degree
6. Bestows
7. "Chicago" star
8. Hand (out)
9. Deep fissure
10. Just when expected
11. Memento
12. Exceeds, as budgeted time
13. Sternward
21. The present
22. "That's what you think!"
26. Darkroom abbr.
28. Iota preceder
30. Knock the socks off
31. Checkout counter item
34. Ice cream amount
36. Discontinuity
38. Cursor mover
39. "Don't move!"
40. Contemporary
41. Doesn't sign off on
42. "I'm impressed!"
43. Part of TGIF
47. Reprimanded
48. Have something
50. Got angry, so to speak
52. Part of PIN
53. Preprogrammed, perhaps
54. Got comfy
56. Adagio, for instance
58. Saint __ and Nevis
61. Great success
62. Gargantuan
63. 27th president
64. Have debt

ACROSS

1. __ Jones Industrial Average
4. Infant's ailment
9. Spaghetti or ziti
14. Early afternoon
15. Coral island
16. Homer's Trojan War epic
17. Speaks frankly
20. Straightens (up)
21. Hand over formally
22. Paradises
23. Very pale
25. Astronaut's insignia
29. Unlit
30. Sore spot
31. Lowly chess pieces
32. Regarding
33. Sums to
34. Speaks frankly
37. Window coverings
39. Earl of tea
40. Puppy sounds
41. Immense
42. Burn slightly
46. Fencing weapon
47. When summer starts
48. Socially smooth
49. Place for protons
51. Some baseball pitches
52. Speaks frankly
57. Kennel club classification
58. Propelled with oars
59. Mother Teresa, for one
60. Reverend Jackson
61. Author Harriet Beecher __
62. Acquire

DOWN

1. Topped, as an "i"
2. Central New York lake
3. Blowtorch wielder
4. Wholesale quantities
5. Elevator pioneer
6. Group offered at auction
7. Under the weather
8. Trite saying
9. __ Piper of Hamelin
10. Estrange
11. Command to Fido
12. Mai __ cocktail
13. Infomercials, e.g.
18. Website connection
19. All-important
23. Plays a part
24. Hunter's weapon
26. On the road
27. Long-running NBC weekend show
28. Wild equine
30. Seeks permission
31. Annoyingly slow
32. Pub beverages
33. Squirrel's hangout
34. "Tall" story
35. Placates
36. Spur, with "on"
37. Salon application
38. One's good name, for short
41. Indulges
42. Spiral shape
43. Ordering for dinner
44. Broad street
45. Take exception to
47. Scribble (down)
48. Leather variety
50. Oceanic movement
51. Scold, with "out"
52. JFK successor
53. Exist
54. Positive response
55. "__ to worry"
56. Early afternoon

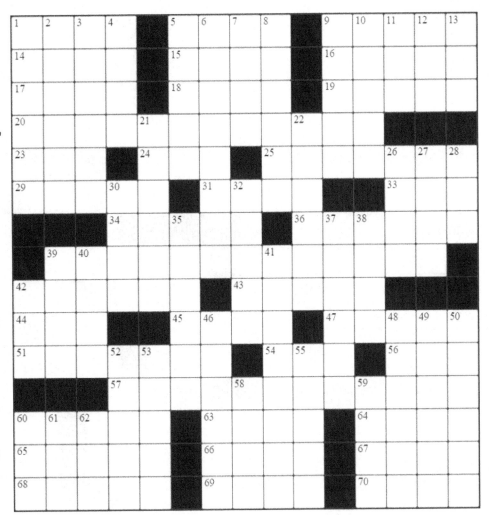

ACROSS

1. Brainchild
5. Unlikely poker winner
9. Weather, in verse
14. Begin to drip
15. Sign on
16. First "Who's Who in the Bible" entry
17. Purina sister brand
18. ___ Republic of Egypt
19. Reacts irritably
20. World's most massive tree
23. Part of RSVP
24. Sunset shade
25. "I Ching" readers
29. Emotionless
31. Right hand, for short
33. Cow's cousin
34. Garlicky sauce
36. With fairness
39. Diva's ostentatious arrival
42. Sunset shade
43. Giant in networking hardware
44. Up on the latest
45. Depend on
47. Utility bill data
51. How poached eggs may be served
54. www.umass.___
56. Postal Creed conjunction
57. Halloween season "Peanuts" subject
60. Isle near Naples
63. Panetta who headed the CIA
64. Olympic pool pathway
65. Primal impulses
66. Not excluded from
67. Societies: Abbr.
68. Annoying one
69. Not otherwise engaged
70. Bygone

DOWN

1. Things seen
2. Remove from a stock exchange
3. Rio Grande city
4. Loads
5. Lunar view
6. Largest of the terriers
7. Persian Gulf land
8. Counters, in a debate
9. Timex alternative
10. Open-sided porch
11. Roth plan
12. Unruly hair
13. Recent USNA grad
21. Vexatious
22. Pictures with posses
26. Coordinate
27. Bit of folklore
28. Kite site
30. Flatbread of India
32. Beginning on
35. City west of Copenhagen
37. Household appliance
38. Grandson of Eve
39. "Silly" expression
40. Deep in thought
41. Starfish habitat
42. "What have we here!"
46. And others, to Antony
48. Eurasian capital
49. Departures
50. Physicist Rutherford
52. Shrek and kin
53. Come to light
55. Journalist/author Dominick
58. Be inclined (to)
59. Sit inelegantly
60. Truncate
61. Take place
62. Sports "Tour" grp.

ACROSS

1. Edge of a cup
4. __ halt to (end)
9. Ecuador neighbor
13. Slice of history
14. Hunter constellation
15. Helpful hints
16. Work wk. start
17. Toy tooter
18. Entices
19. Jump __ (follow a popular cause)
22. Eight, on a sundial
23. Large bodies of water
24. Faux __ (minor mistake)
26. Extreme happiness
30. Orator's delivery
32. With a roof, as stadiums
35. Fence entryway
36. Jump __ (decide hastily)
41. Mystical glow
42. Run __ of (clash with)
43. Uses a coffee mill
46. Stain on an artist's smock
51. Word on a penny
52. Very funny person
55. Prefix for dynamic
56. Jump __ (begin enthusiastically)
61. Loosen, as laces
62. Google competitor
63. Bar bill
64. Parts of a stairway
65. Inventor Howe
66. Language suffix
67. Cryptographic writing
68. Job openings
69. Color of rare steak

DOWN

1. Delete
2. Wryly amusing
3. "Praying" insect
4. Pepsi rival
5. Typical Saudi
6. Entertainer Minnelli
7. Lake birds
8. Battery terminal
9. Electrical outlet insert
10. Spaniard or Swede
11. Stages, as a historical battle
12. Battleship letters
15. Envelope fastener
20. Box office success
21. Used to be
25. That woman
27. Commotion
28. Dad's boy
29. Community pool site
31. Swelled head
33. Santa's assistant
34. Pairs of singers

36. Become
37. Pointed properly
38. Tuna container
39. Have an evening meal
40. Under the weather
41. Long, long __
44. Helps with the dishes
45. Take a chair
47. Clumsy person
48. Move unsteadily
49. Pants pleat, for example
50. Place of rapid growth
53. Emphatic agreement
54. Batting game for tots
57. Help with the dishes
58. It's east of Indiana
59. Perfectly
60. Cowpoke's ride
61. L.A. campus

ACROSS

1. Charitable gift
5. Generic poodle name
9. Latter-day "Toodle-oo!"
14. Unrattled
15. Nation on the Arabian Sea
16. In reserve
17. Rather late lunch time
19. Watch a TV series all day
20. Crucial tennis situation
21. Did an airport screener's job
22. Luau fare
23. Org. for entrepreneurs
24. Fumble in the dark
28. Burrito seller on wheels
34. Rio Grande city
36. Overly easygoing
37. Big Apple's Arthur __ Stadium
38. Commando weapons
39. Certain saline solution
41. One-on-one contest
42. Tugboat sound
43. Movie-popcorn holder
44. Shaped like fusilli pasta
46. Cube inventor
49. Prone to backtalk
50. Pack animal
51. Tabloid transport
53. Hose attachment
57. Stir-fry fare
62. Uptrending shopping
63. Toy for jumping
64. Young fella
65. Inflatable vessel
66. "Toy Story" kid
67. Things at hand
68. Numbered musical work
69. Cabinet dept. head

DOWN

1. Reaches a decision
2. Actor Rob
3. No longer worth discussing
4. Spill (over)
5. Four-page sheet
6. "Leave that to me"
7. Something proven
8. Prepare, as a press
9. On-the-move maze solver
10. Where water buffalo roam
11. Barely visible
12. Head start
13. Swamp grass
18. Handled a hassle
21. PlayStation alternatives
23. Do an airport screener's job
24. Muscle strengthened by squats
25. Household blade
26. Belted constellation
27. Sauce with pine nuts
29. Courtroom defense
30. Rim-to-hub lines
31. Take over by force
32. A steal
33. Pop singer Clarkson
35. Thickheaded
40. Rib-joint applications
45. Agricultural equipment
47. Public-road race
48. Action-movie art
52. Picks up, as a bill
53. Cozy spot
54. "Then again . . ." in texts
55. Grey of westerns
56. California wines, for short
57. Hotel freebie
58. Bake-sale orgs.
59. German article
60. Adapter designation
61. Blue-bottle vodka brand
63. Country club instructor

Puzzle #66

66

ACROSS

1. WWII surrender celebration
6. Mosque leader
10. Few
14. Author Jong
15. City near Carson City
16. Campus courtyard
17. Blacksmith's iron block
18. Prefix for social
19. Commando weapons
20. Inquiry with an unjustified assumption
23. Feel bad about
24. Ado
25. In the matter of
28. AFL's union partner
31. Santa costume part
35. Blueprint detail
36. Prophet
39. Armed conflict
40. Prepared for a trip
43. How Germans say "I"
44. Doctrines
45. __ and crafts
46. Jai alai basket
48. Collector's goal
49. Herbal brews
50. Bad habit
53. List-ending abbr.
55. Captain's acceleration order
62. Civil rights activist Parks
63. Opinion survey
64. Coffeehouse order
65. Covered-wagon beasts
66. Line of rotation
67. Pop singer __ John
68. Polar explorer Richard
69. Market covered by CNBC
70. Was snoozing

DOWN

1. Cutlet meat
2. Inventor Rubik
3. Prima donna
4. Woodstock-era music
5. Conn. school
6. Baghdad's land
7. List of entrées
8. Starts a poker hand
9. Damp
10. Knight trainee
11. Greek liqueur
12. Most important
13. Newspaper execs.
21. Solve, as a secret message
22. Lama land
25. Jellied garnish
26. Place to park
27. Computer troubleshooters
29. 6 Down neighbor
30. Watering holes
32. Cognizant
33. Dreadlocks wearer
34. Wedding gown, for one
37. Adorable
38. On the roster
41. Online sales, for short
42. Miscellaneous
47. Cable channel airing vintage sitcoms
51. Cable channel airing the Senate
52. Strong adhesive
54. Folk stories
55. Cunning
56. Web surfer
57. Students at 5 Down
58. Besides that
59. Suffix for luncheon
60. At the summit of
61. Food-can damage
62. Steal from

ACROSS

1. Past masters
5. Honda rival
10. Voice of Daffy and Bugs
13. Rude awakening
14. Awakening cause, often
15. Doha dignitary
17. Wheeled whistleblower
20. Made off with
21. Taste testers
22. Actor Channing
24. Fork feature
25. Kid
26. Lunar plain
27. Poke fun at
29. Philosopher Descartes
30. Modern conference venue
32. Took pits from
34. Household whistleblower
36. Bank (on)
39. Kids
43. Former couples
44. Befit
45. Point of view, so to speak
46. Paramedic skill
47. Microwave sound
49. WALL-E, for instance
50. Math course
52. Raucous sound
54. Athletics whistleblower
58. Corn holder
59. Usher to the parlor
60. Quaint oath
61. Shade of suede
62. Moved gradually
63. With 56 Down, dinner invitation

DOWN

1. Nitewear
2. Foolish talk
3. Faux fat
4. Oscars and Emmys
5. Commercial complex
6. Salve ingredient
7. Singer/actor Efron
8. "Change the subject"
9. Mideast capital
10. Prefix meaning "beyond"
11. Radiated
12. Hot prospect
16. Took a time out
18. Melanie, to Dakota
19. World Cup cheer
22. Showtime sister channel
23. Sound of relief
24. "Pencils down, please"
27. Despicable one
28. Kung Pao chicken cooker
29. Retro audio adjective
31. ___ Faire (Elizabethan festival)
32. Tabular tidbit
33. 90° shape
35. Texter's "Enough details"
36. Some lattes
37. Take advantage of
38. Vine-covered walkway
40. Big name in eggs
41. Desilu acquired its studios
42. To date
44. Airtight
47. Merchants' assn.
48. Obliterate
49. UK's Gulf War contingent
51. Venerable prep school
52. Party spread
53. First verb in Antony's big speech
55. Trip segment
56. See 63 Across
57. Journal VIPs

ACROSS

1. Con game
5. Musical conclusion
9. Concert ticket remnants
14. It's east of Indiana
15. Primates without tails
16. Wigwam relative
17. Clothes, informally
18. Interoffice message
19. Devoured
20. Fact in a court document
23. Historical period
24. University email suffix
25. Turkey's capital
29. Airport rental
31. Office seekers, for short
35. Nary a soul
36. Grand parties
38. Pied Piper follower
39. Small cellophane roll
42. Subj. for some immigrants
43. Assumed name
44. Shampoo bottle instruction
45. Center of government
47. Picnic invader
48. Sushi side dish
49. Got the gold medal
51. Physician's nickname
52. Credit union investment
60. Social gathering
61. Not that much
62. Bona fide
64. Bit of color
65. Sound of mind
66. Doing nothing
67. More eccentric
68. Little fellow
69. Something essential

DOWN

1. Grass bought in rolls
2. Buddy
3. Verdi masterwork
4. A majority of
5. Film-set machine
6. 3 Down, for example
7. Showroom sample
8. No earlier than
9. General's horse
10. Saucer's partner
11. No later than
12. Foamy beverage
13. Fax button
21. Nun with a Nobel Prize
22. Televised again
25. Chips in
26. Of the Vikings
27. Arboreal Aussie
28. Raggedy doll
29. Sapphire measure
30. Foamy beverages
32. One of the 15 Across
33. Run out, as subscriptions
34. Rodeo beast
36. Make progress
37. Far from lenient
40. Backup strategy
41. Metal in bronze
46. Sudden spasm
48. Small beard
50. Western film
51. Beverage
52. Governor's rejection
53. Gung-ho
54. Rip apart
55. Be durable
56. Cyberseller's site
57. Ireland, in poetry
58. Relinquish
59. Self-help author Carnegie
63. Spearheaded

ACROSS

1. Wander idly
4. Slides off course
9. Group heard in "Mamma Mia!"
13. Sporting blade
15. Photographer Adams
16. Rate of speed
17. US Women's Open org.
18. Backyard barbecue brand
19. Attention to propriety
20. Motivational system
23. Guinness product
24. Discreet approval
25. Followed the trail
27. Drapery feature
29. Needing rinsing, perhaps
33. Start for cycle
34. Place (down)
36. "I shoulda worn a coat!"
37. Poetic measures
38. Plastic toy with a handbag
42. Venetian valedictory
43. Reservoir creator
44. Someone Adam hadn't
45. Code for O'Hare
46. It's south of Molokai
48. Entertainer Abdul
52. Disappear slowly
54. Alphabetic trio
56. Prefix like centri-
57. It's right for a light kite
62. Best Picture Oscar film for 2012
63. O'Connor's court successor
64. Avia rival
65. Scanned through
66. Spec episode
67. Moderate pace
68. Whse. goods
69. Fire sign
70. Shearing candidate

DOWN

1. Medicinal medium
2. Outrage
3. Stage of progression
4. Dealt with
5. Works with clay
6. Book ID
7. Accomplishment
8. Pros' cameras
9. The end of "Evita"
10. Orange pekoe, e.g.
11. Had words
12. Quick to learn
14. Linguist's ability
21. Standing by
22. Commandments pronoun
26. Morse code sound
28. To boot
30. Only Columbia grad to become President
31. Creative works

32. High-school gala
35. Character in many Star Wars films
37. Homeland Security org.
38. Depicted faithfully
39. Home inspector's concern
40. Earth tone
41. Amplify, so to speak
42. Cedar Rapids campus
46. Kate's "Titanic" costar
47. "Does this work for you?"
49. Rainout decider
50. Stay out of sight
51. Mag rep's quote
53. Part of LED
55. Govt. debt instrument
58. Brief refreshers
59. Slight of frame
60. About 35 ounces
61. Where a rudder is
62. Offshoot

ACROSS

1. Alphabetize
5. More to the point
10. Wild guess
14. Creme-filled cookie
15. About to cry
16. Remarkable thing
17. Departed
20. Sports stadium
21. Set of luggage
22. Mischievous sprites
25. Fruit-tree grove
28. Loosens, as shoelaces
29. Prez after Harry
30. Big brass instrument
31. Astounds
32. Muffin ingredient
34. Poorly lit
35. Precede in a line
39. Clumsy one
42. Final Four org.
43. Mythical giant
47. New Mexico art community
49. Edge of a cup
50. Late-night flight
51. Drive-sharing group
53. Was jealous of
54. Transgressions
55. Very mean
56. "Exactly!"
62. Money succeeding the mark
63. Fuming
64. Beverages brewed from bags
65. "Don't delete" notation
66. Antic
67. Canine cry

DOWN

1. Note after fa
2. Mined mineral
3. Basketball official
4. Adding up
5. Acropolis city
6. Hammer parts
7. Spanish appetizer
8. Go wrong
9. Bagel alternative
10. Trivial
11. Madame of wax museums
12. Pub order
13. Train alternative
18. Checks for size
19. Apple computer
22. "Gloomy" guy
23. Ottawa's prov.
24. A/C measure
25. Gumbo veggie
26. Slugger's stat, for short
27. River blocker
29. Steel girder
33. At no time
36. Quotation puzzle
37. Pellet precipitation
38. Faithfulness
39. Nonprescription: Abbr.
40. Road service org.
41. "Definitely!"
44. Vietnamese New Year
45. Ensign's 56 Down
46. Homer Simpson's neighbor
48. Faucet
50. Computer-network device
52. Yoko __
53. Box for oranges
55. British bloke
56. "Certainly"
57. Half of a double play
58. __ la la
59. "Golly!"
60. "2001" computer
61. Recipe meas.

ACROSS

1. Symbol of QANTAS
6. "Veni"
11. French noble
14. Henry Ford's son
15. "Interstellar" director
16. Elementary school trio
17. Embroidery hobby
19. Vanity center
20. France, formerly
21. German city
23. Rhode Island city
27. "La Mer" composer
29. Plato's home
30. Language of Libya
31. Midwest hub
32. Fierce look
33. DJIA stock
36. Joey on "Friends"
37. Shimmery fabric
38. Weimar wife
39. Helpful connections
40. Early evening
41. Is missing
42. Austrian symphonist
44. Where bills are kept
45. Power source of a sort
47. Shopkeepers
48. Swiss mathematician
49. Sci-fi knight
50. Prefix for center
51. Sum-thing special in arithmetic
58. Snug retreat
59. Deal maker
60. Excessive
61. Be a spectator at
62. Bright crayon colors
63. Pillow material

DOWN

1. Range of knowledge
2. Metrical tribute
3. Enzyme ending
4. Took by the hand
5. Depleted
6. Discussion contribution
7. Unflappable
8. '70s ring king
9. Guy
10. Ugandan city
11. Opera-house section
12. Strong impulses
13. Pal
18. Facial features
22. Fashion designer Anna
23. Actress Watts
24. Fictional Frome
25. Classic TV game show
26. Saucy
27. Draw water from
28. Warrant
30. Fiddle with
32. Auction accessory
34. Cake specialist
35. Requirements
37. Win over
38. Raking season
40. Peabody's toon partner
41. Big name in French crystal
43. Hole in one
44. Unites
45. House papers
46. Kolkata coin
47. Schools of thought
49. Islamic spirit
52. Era
53. Nat __ (cable channel, for short)
54. Prefix for cycle
55. Mix in
56. Bewail
57. Suffix for sonnet

Puzzle #72

ACROSS

1. Lowest face card
5. 14 Across' region, for short
10. Apple's tablet
14. Pac-12 sch.
15. São ___, Brazil
16. Soy product in stir-fry
17. Amateur photographer
19. "Shoo!"
20. Giggling sound
21. Diplomat
23. Little boys
25. Biblical boat builder
26. Stave off
29. Scottish hat
32. Take from a pet shelter
35. Beauty cream additive
36. Ripped to pieces
38. Teachers' org.
39. High-tech collision preventer
42. Stiller or Kingsley
43. Rum __ ice cream
44. Peaceful
45. Opening remarks
47. Collarless shirt
48. In disarray
49. Kite's end
51. Render unusable
53. Haphazard
57. Stand at attention
61. Collaborative website
62. Beeches and birches
64. Imitated
65. Really enjoy
66. Slanting type: Abbr.
67. Great quantities
68. Hints of what's to come
69. __ buco (Italian entrée)

DOWN

1. Fair-minded
2. Massage target
3. Whodunit hint
4. Soprano Battle
5. Go quickly
6. Dinghy propeller
7. Shape for 16 Across
8. Homecoming guest
9. Gain online access
10. "Alas . . ."
11. Native American title character of a Disney film
12. Worship from ___
13. Obligation
18. Greenish blue
22. Needing rinsing
24. "Cut that out!"
26. Torah authority
27. Talk host DeGeneres
28. "I see what you mean"
30. Popped up
31. Field of work
33. Banana discards
34. Country singer Wynette
36. Air marshal's org.
37. Admiral's org.
40. "Star Wars" robot
41. Possible outcome
46. Kayaking challenge
48. Coin-making factory
50. Rodeo rope
52. Manual readers
53. Heavy blow
54. Slimming procedure, briefly
55. Hoax
56. "__ a good one!"
58. Vet patients
59. Herbal brews
60. Scandinavian capital
63. Quixote title

Puzzle #73

ACROSS

1. Last stop before home
6. Chamber music group
11. Site of Gump heroics
14. Backer of the Bulldogs
15. Oslo native's homeland
16. Shout like "Bravo!"
17. Tarantino comedy crime caper
19. App glitch
20. Addition column
21. "Wait a minute . . ."
22. City near Cremona
24. Mason's tool
26. Wombat cousin
28. Wall-tile descriptor
32. Artist fond of lilies
35. Confront
36. Read Across America Day sponsor
37. Eiffel Tower, essentially
38. Uses leverage
40. Make known
41. Unalterable
42. Important stretches
43. Far from windy
44. Players getting byes, often
48. Lawbreakers, so to speak
49. Panoramas
52. Cuban base, familiarly
54. Title given to Poitier
55. Go sprawling
57. Response to a bailiff
58. Michael Keaton film of '88
62. Floral welcome
63. Boot out
64. "Beverly Hillbillies" star
65. Indelible-ink design, for short
66. Melodramatic
67. Crawls (with)

DOWN

1. Keyboard slip
2. Frequented spot
3. Not as hale
4. Unwraps eagerly
5. Telephone trio
6. At the ready
7. French fragrance firm
8. Part of TNT
9. Vanity
10. A bit after the hour
11. Obvious choice
12. Scholarship source, perhaps
13. Prefix for phone
18. "Uh-huh"
23. In-flight stat.
25. Rainy
26. Slapper starter
27. Lofty lines
29. Faulty
30. Pink Panther collectibles
31. Close kin of cabbage
32. Niagara Falls by-product
33. Deep-fried carnival treat
34. Lacking the motivation
38. Attend Eton, e.g.
39. Florida major leaguers
40. Lab glassware
42. Dons judge's garb
43. Manning stats
45. Sleep study acronym
46. How villains behave
47. Limerick's land
50. Ascend
51. Attack command
52. __-edged (best-quality)
53. Inspiration
54. Aerobics class prop
56. Highlighters, for instance
59. "Outer" prefix
60. Clean Water Act administrator
61. Airbus product

ACROSS

1. Performs like Kanye
5. Keglers' org.
8. Lengthy tale
12. Word-of-mouth
13. Carbonated drink flavor
14. Source of ancient fables
15. Harp on an issue
18. Former
19. Married couples
20. Paving material
21. Capone's nemesis
23. Under the weather
24. Beast of burden
25. Mexican folded food
27. Group of seats
30. Begin a hand
33. Old pros
35. Tour leader
37. Secluded setting
40. Compose, as prose
41. Unlocked
42. Supports for eyeglasses
43. "I should say __!"
44. Moccasin or sandal
46. Brought about
48. From __ Z
49. "Darn it!"
51. Cup border
54. Emergency phone link
58. Isolated region
60. Was punctual
62. Exit the premises
63. Garden entrance
64. Camper's heater
65. Run leisurely
66. Many mos.
67. Tinkers (with)

DOWN

1. Metallic factory worker
2. Sports venue
3. Less tanned
4. Wood strip
5. Sponge holes
6. Crunchy sandwich, for short
7. Sounds relieved
8. South Korean capital
9. With no warranty
10. Part of "GWTW"
11. Tenants' dwellings: Abbr.
13. Charges towards
14. Comment of regret
16. Containers for recyclables
17. Lengthy tale
22. Immersed, as a tea bag
24. Zillions
26. ". . . even __ speak"
27. Morning TV talk host
28. Aroma
29. Makes moist
30. Elevator button
31. 100 German cents
32. Keep __ (persist)
34. Tail end of a sneeze
36. Previously owned
38. Celebratory
39. Slow tempo
45. Sharpen, as skills
47. Scratcher's target
48. Still in the game
50. Tenants' payments
51. Dashboard device
52. Tusk material
53. Doles (out)
54. Office passageway
55. Best-selling cookie
56. Ensnare
57. Feeling tense
59. Exited
61. Rower's blade

ACROSS

1. Renown
5. "Hold that down!"
10. Gulf War projectile
14. Meager
15. Keep busy
16. Gershwin creation
17. Fighting force
18. "Cheers" server
19. Abbey alcove
20. "California Dreamin' " voice
23. Frat letter
24. Water carrier
25. Deduce
27. India's Capital territory
29. Rescue squad VIP
31. Tasseled topper
32. Meddle
36. HS equivalency exams
37. Literary nickname
40. Froth
41. Ecstatic joy
42. Ace
43. Droning sound
44. Uneasy feeling
48. Condor's home
50. Bit of progress
53. Gibraltar beast
54. '30s bank robber
58. Celestial spheres
59. WWII threat
60. Sit against
61. Strike out
62. Pick up on
63. Crush to a pulp
64. Genesis 2 locale
65. Herd member
66. Pretty long time

DOWN

1. Combusted
2. Make bubbly
3. Anteater, for one
4. Irish New Age singer
5. Chocolate source
6. Build up
7. Sip slowly
8. Spot in a chain
9. Greenish blue
10. Spot
11. Preference, so to speak
12. Teetering
13. Low grade
21. Security Council member
22. Set off
26. Bldg. makeup
28. Shorts supports
29. Prepare for viewing
30. Card of courses
33. Via, briefly
34. 500 sheets
35. Plate cleaner
36. Singer Stefani
37. Pedigreed
38. So cute
39. Jam flavor
40. Hotel amenity
43. "Watch where you're going!"
45. Big talker
46. Half of a couple
47. Decimal division
49. "A Doll's House" playwright
50. Breakfast pastry
51. Heckle
52. Begin upon
55. Ado
56. Aid partner
57. Priest cited by Nash
58. Keats creation

Puzzle #76

ACROSS

1. Biblical song
6. Alan of "M*A*S*H"
10. Do the backstroke
14. Variety show
15. Place to do the backstroke
16. British bloke
17. Last Greek letter
18. Just hanging around
20. Miss America's understudy
22. Battleship designation
23. Bit of barbecue
24. Changed into
29. Lowest royal-flush card
30. "Spring forward" period: Abbr.
33. Farewell in Hawaii
34. Male deer
36. Farewell in Florence
37. Ship's executive officer
40. Gross, to a tot
41. Gung-ho about
42. Prepared a filet
43. Pig's place
44. Flavor enhancer initials
45. Yellow songbird
46. Stand __ (take no cards)
47. Debt reminder
49. Teammate who rarely plays
56. Most reliable
58. Oscar actress Julianne
59. Historical periods
60. Whodunit hint
61. Locale of the Louvre
62. Electrical line
63. Theater level
64. Mattress covering

DOWN

1. University teacher, for short
2. Prefix for circle
3. State with confidence
4. Drags around
5. Food avoided by vegans
6. Very high grade
7. Lake birds
8. Tire out completely
9. Clark Kent, to Superman
10. Cancel, as a space mission
11. Use an eggbeater on
12. 007 creator Fleming
13. Gasoline consumption stat.
19. Ireland nickname
21. Regret
24. Underlying principle
25. Choose by ballot
26. Overly confident
27. Sailor's greeting
28. Guy
29. Crunchy Mexican food
30. Prince William's mom
31. More rational
32. "Hot" winter drink
34. Perform a ballad
35. Explosive initials
36. "Let's get moving!"
38. Part of DC
39. Wharton deg.
44. Hotel housekeeper
45. Mongrel
46. Crescent or new moon
47. Discussion point
48. Aquatic mammal
49. Split apart, as paper
50. Sandwich shop
51. Little rascals
52. Lexicographer Webster
53. 1990s vice president
54. Water beside Buffalo
55. Take five
56. Stitch up
57. Prefix for cycle

ACROSS

1. Poultry purchase
6. Polish partner
10. Custard tart
14. Grand display
15. Jorge's hand
16. Top-drawer
17. Slip fillers
18. Source of some ice creams' crunch
19. Biblical preposition
20. "Clueless" director
23. Damsel
24. On its way
25. Cowpoke's catcher
28. Concentrate chemically
30. "Self" starter
31. Activist Chavez
35. Calendar abbr.
36. Good: Lat.
37. With 39 Across, "SNL" regular, 1999-2006
39. See 37 Across
41. Post-takeoff announcements
42. Lummox
45. Out of port
46. Poetic adverb
47. Dressy occasions
50. Work clay
52. Abbey area
53. Accord
57. Dickensian defendant
60. Jesse Jackson once wore it
62. Limerick land
63. Unearth
64. Cashmere, for instance
65. The Bard's "any day now"
66. Entertain
67. Not decent
68. Fresh-mouthed
69. Ancient tablet holder

DOWN

1. Conspiracy
2. Wine feature
3. Entreats
4. Swear words
5. 11 Wall St. institution
6. Fumigates
7. Mag for moms and dads
8. Passivity
9. Plane or level
10. Regional beasts
11. Dark horses
12. Aesopian insect
13. "New" beginning
21. TV forensic franchise
22. Not up to par
26. Subsequently
27. City near Council Bluffs
28. Grammy-winning Dr.
29. Inc., in the UK
31. Rural swimming spot
32. Bolted down
33. Emerald City visitor
34. Sighed sounds
36. Dracula's alter ego
38. Southeast Asian language
40. Dorm VIPs
43. Louisiana candy
44. Montezuma, for one
47. Vitamin regulator
48. Thumbs-up
49. Initiated
51. Get __ of (obtain)
53. Top-drawer
54. Cattle from Scotland
55. Bring about
56. Sorts
58. Gather in
59. First of all
60. Cobbler's punch
61. Hostile force

★★☆

ACROSS

1. Deep sleeps
6. Baton Rouge sch.
9. Pied Piper follower
12. Give a speech
13. Playthings
14. Japanese martial art
15. Analog watch part
17. Get __ the ground floor
18. Beyond what's needed
19. Taxi ride price
21. Gasoline holder
23. In pursuit of
24. Miss Muffet's seat
28. Manicurist's abrasive
31. Milky gems
32. Become well again
33. After the buzzer
37. What Italians call their capital
38. Italian resort isle
39. UCLA part: Abbr.
40. Small bills
41. Fighting force
42. Higher than
43. Typical native of India
45. Shorthand experts
46. Tourist magnet
49. Water around a castle
51. Household tasks
54. Car radio buttons
59. Visionary
60. Lipton powdery product
62. Scored perfectly on
63. Slapstick missiles
64. Sees socially
65. Norm: Abbr.
66. Mineral spring
67. Leaves in awe

DOWN

1. Expense
2. Lunchbox dessert item
3. PC alternatives
4. On the summit of
5. Legislative bodies
6. Mauna __
7. Harmonize, for short
8. Egg-grading agcy.
9. Charge toward
10. Like a lot
11. Copier powder
13. At that time
14. Oil-change chain
16. "Darn it!"
20. Tavern
22. Say nothing
24. Barcelona bull
25. Knowledgeable about
26. Renown
27. Arithmetic drill aid
29. Nativity scene figure
30. Inventor Whitney
32. Difficult
34. Uncredited: Abbr.
35. TV room device
36. Days before holidays
38. Is able to
42. Is present at
44. Novelist Fleming
45. __ Lee cakes
46. Western elevations
47. Standing tall
48. Religious belief
50. Chooses, with "for"
52. Quick swims
53. Quick cut
55. PDQ, in the OR
56. Caesar's rebuke
57. Young adult
58. Bratty talk
61. Europe-Africa separator

ACROSS

1. Staying power, so to speak
5. Austen novel
9. Brain work
13. Beast battled by Hercules
14. Animal park barrier
15. Persians, for example
16. Spring sign
17. Has no presence
18. "I heard you the first time"
19. . . . on the links
22. Berliner's eight
23. Fog companion
24. Considering, as an opportunity
27. SpaceX partner
29. Conjunction in rebus puzzles
31. Not-shabby filling
32. Endeavored (to)
35. At-bat stat
36. Garrison
37. . . . at the casino
41. Fourth planet
42. Brink
43. Fee schedule
44. Contents of some cartridges
45. Tourney pass
46. 34 Down title jumper
48. Marquee line
50. Offense to a sense
52. Sardine cousin
56. . . . at a convenience store
59. Some long-term investments
61. Sleekly designed
62. Depend (on)
63. Pub offering, perhaps
64. Cats and dogs, metaphorically
65. Transpire
66. Email folder
67. Quarry
68. Small strings

DOWN

1. Poetic descriptor
2. "Downton Abbey" daughter
3. "Wait until you hear this!"
4. Ornamental band
5. Mrs. Iago
6. Biblical "stranger in a strange land"
7. Minnesota neighbor
8. Routing abbr.
9. "Gift of the Magi" device
10. Go mano a mano
11. Driving force
12. Call (for)
13. A few laughs
20. Mantra chants
21. Poetic preposition
25. Earliest Icelanders
26. Roman Empire invaders
28. Toothpaste box abbr.
30. Feel off
32. Own up to
33. Farsi speaker
34. Whom an American humor prize is named for
35. Ham holder
36. Golfer's target
38. Spanish king
39. Learn by accident, perhaps
40. One way to sway
45. Founding Father, familiarly
46. Fraud, for instance
47. Studio for most Astaire/Rogers films
49. "Hungarian Rhapsodies" composer
51. Spooky
53. That being so
54. Builder of Jason's ship
55. Colorist
57. Infield covering
58. What "you" once was
59. Measures of brightness
60. Regret

ACROSS

1. Was in possession of
4. Animal fat for frying
8. Pay tribute to
13. Give a darn
14. Cake decorator
15. Get married in secret
16. Door-to-door cosmetics seller
17. Jai __
18. Flood barrier
19. "Half" prefix for final
20. Large bag for potatoes
22. Tooth covering
24. Skinny
25. Shout scornfully at
27. Teaching session
32. Roadside stopover
35. Stare at
38. "Pay __ mind"
39. Region
40. Say "not guilty," perhaps
41. In __ of (rather than)
42. Observed
43. Shade trees
44. Ohio tire city
45. Throws softly
47. __-control (willpower)
49. Misplace
52. Make a choice
56. Camper's shelter
61. Honolulu's locale
62. Red as __ (embarrassed)
63. A Great Lake
64. Small songbird
65. Chalkboard material
66. Champagne or Chianti
67. Otherwise
68. Long sandwiches
69. Appear to be
70. Trio after Q

DOWN

1. Place of safety
2. Scent
3. Casual pants
4. Apt (to)
5. Citizens' rights org.
6. Brings up, as children
7. Hole-boring tool
8. "I need assistance"
9. Bullring cheers
10. __ Scotia, Canada
11. Oil cartel
12. Smell bad
13. Job for a detective
21. Was feeling poorly
23. Snakelike fish
26. Bun or bagel
28. Decorative artificial bloom
29. Blend with a spoon
30. __'clock (hour after noon)
31. Person, place, or thing
32. Ship's pole

33. Black-and-white cookie
34. Golfer's pegs
36. Ruby or diamond
37. Young lady
40. Mexican coins
44. Pub beverage
46. Makes very happy
48. Regard highly
50. One-pot beef dishes
51. Spooky
53. British noblemen
54. Pirate's treasure holder
55. Song
56. __ register (store's money holder)
57. Up to the task
58. Close-by
59. Presidential rejection
60. Three hours before noon

Puzzle #81

ACROSS

1. Portrayed
4. "Curious George" guy
7. "That's terrible!"
10. Render less perfect
13. Rescue pro
14. Hack
15. Beaver St.
16. Second-biggest bird
17. Class competition
18. It may move you
19. Munich-based manufacturer
20. Diamond St.
21. False ally
23. Abridged, perhaps
25. Albertan NHL team
26. Hardy follower
27. Symbol of virtue
28. Vast body
29. CHALLENGE TO A SUN-BATHER
31. Caustic
32. "That's impressive!"
33. Dish towel material
34. KICK OUT A COMEDIAN
37. Cleaning products
39. Sched. board datum
40. Draft choice
44. HAS A LEAKY TUB
46. Consequently
47. Oil Market Report producer
48. __ Gatos, CA
49. What rain does on wax
50. "Elementary Seismology" author
52. Guatemala's national bird
53. In accordance with
54. Adjective ending
55. "That's terrible!"
56. Laudatory lines
57. Low "número"
58. Easter preceder
59. Taking after
60. "I should think __"
61. Octane Booster brand
62. End for some long lunches
63. What might soak your morning paper
64. It sounds like "air"

DOWN

1. Penguin feature
2. Grade school anthem
3. Heinz Field player
4. Pub
5. Physicals, for instance
6. Don't allow
7. Initial Cub Scout rank
8. Well-protected, as a warship
9. Hacked
10. Help to settle
11. Fingerspelling skill
12. Decide formally
22. COOL COOKIE QUANTITY
24. PROTESTER'S TEMPO
26. Sly laughs
29. Web-crawling software
30. Here: Lat.
32. Ad enticement
35. Wide-area alert
36. "Saison humide"
37. Wise
38. Undiversified, as a farm
41. Goalpost locale
42. Galápagos owner
43. Surfeited
44. Full literary collection
45. "Carmen" character
46. Barnyard sound
49. Cornet cousin
51. Hair treatment
52. Frisbee field, perhaps

ACROSS

1. Poet pal of Manet
11. Small, thin child
15. First Canadian woman with a #1 solo U.S. song
16. Mariachi subject
17. 100+, most certainly
18. Nearly impossible
19. "The Ultimate Beauty Tool"
20. First name of a Rock Hall of Fame "key inductee"
21. Is parasitic
23. Williams-Sonoma's HQ
25. Bed attachments
26. Knock off or over
27. Moves energetically
28. Macaroni
29. 51 Across et al.
33. Where Fermi went to college
34. Angelic narrator of Haydn's "Creation"
35. Support for Atlético Madrid
36. With 37 Across, introduction to marketing
37. See 36 Across
38. Scary movies, often
40. Clear out
41. What shortcuts sidestep
42. Something found in a "Ben-Hur" bank
43. Google News category
45. Hematology adjective
49. Hang together
50. Weekly initiator
51. Newfoundland first seen in a 1904 play
52. Salutes with rhythm
53. Onetime Leonardo on "Teenage Mutant Ninja Turtles"
56. Storm warning of a sort
57. Piquant cookie ingredient
58. One way to say this
59. Takeoff points

DOWN

1. "Olde Tyme" drink brand
2. Shark singing "Tonight Quintet"
3. Free, in a way
4. How some Oreos are eaten
5. "Yesterday's Feelings" rock genre
6. Rock music?
7. Region bordering the Avon
8. They're usually tapped after work
9. Shot shirt, maybe
10. Contoured camera components
11. Minor charges
12. Compression candidate
13. Court crybaby
14. Trade-show issuance
22. One in a pack
24. Get going
25. Crash scene?
27. Confute
29. Comprehensive
30. Trios starting numbers
31. Its mascot is the fireball Burnie
32. Crib or cook
33. Talk down to
36. Asian territory in Risk
38. "I try" elicitor
39. Large liners
41. "Égée" or "Noire"
44. Next automaker to go public after Ford
45. Weaving material
46. Blinding things
47. Unease
48. Goes on and on
50. __ Bell (Kremlin attraction)
54. With 55 Down and "Canaan," "Exodus" lead role
55. See 54 Down

ACROSS

1. Become rough
5. It's south of Samoa
10. Indistinctness
14. Verdi masterwork
15. Cream-colored
16. Welsh form of John
17. START OF A QUESTION FROM "B.C."
20. Supreme Court name
21. Telejournalist Dobbs
22. Place for alpacas
23. Source for green eggs
25. Media statistician Silver
27. British broth ingredient
30. Maritime title
33. More than half of us all
34. Curb, with "in"
35. "Agnus __"
37. PART 2 OF QUESTION
38. PART 3 OF QUESTION
39. END OF QUESTION
40. Blunder
41. Comic routines
43. Swank biopic
45. Board with a thumbhole
47. Low A
48. Stock villain in Gothic fiction
49. It may be marching
50. Lectured
53. START OF ANSWER
55. Conspiracy
59. END OF ANSWER
62. Vigor
63. Web-footed mammal
64. Horoscope beast
65. Geneticist portrayer in "Jurassic World"
66. App clientele
67. Sherwood Forest trees

DOWN

1. Crow sounds

2. Jaunty greeting
3. Arabian gulf
4. Brain lobe
5. Idiosyncrasy
6. Egg outlines
7. Proscribed practice
8. Rolling baseball
9. Big name in Objectivism
10. He financed a Clara Bow documentary
11. Voracious
12. Name on the cover of "Wild Horse Mesa"
13. Wraps up
18. Irish statesman De Valera
19. Dinette descriptor
24. Ones: Fr.
26. End of Horner's boast
27. Fashioned
28. Encroach on
29. Possible bridal wear

30. Spring up
31. Allan-__
32. Kosher
36. Watson exclamation
38. Pulls in
39. Opposite of "rigid"
41. Engender
42. "What was __ think?"
43. Coin collectors' org.
44. Hash up
46. Fondness
49. Recycling facility's machine
50. Shoot out
51. Columbus inspiration
52. "The Good Earth" character
54. __ Modern (London art gallery)
56. Cost of leaving
57. Depiction on an Emmy
58. Smartphone part
60. Slip in a pot
61. Watson et al.

Puzzle #84

ACROSS

1. Literally, "sense of touch"
5. Camel's hump, to a naturalist
15. Launches in the news, for short
16. 2009 Lady Gaga tune certified 10-times platinum
17. Org. that checks trailers
18. Unimpressive clip
19. Brilliant swimmer
21. Personal guide
22. Close one, these days
23. Labyrinth setting
24. Go through
26. Falls off
27. Tries to soak up
29. Ill-gotten
31. Second-opinion introducer
32. Impatient inquiry
35. Whom MacArthur called "my best soldiers"
40. Layered dessert
41. Entry point
42. Sound happy
44. Toddler's "Take it away!"
46. Petitions
47. Sunless-tanning brand
49. "The Men Who Stare at Goats" subject
50. Constellation depicted with rising smoke
51. Frito-Lay's Texas base
53. High country
55. Queequeg et al.
58. Considerably
59. Quelling words
60. Very powerful predator
61. Demure drinker of the Baby Boomer era
62. Cluster

DOWN

1. Only sophomore to win the Heisman Trophy
2. Grab
3. Ticket distribution center
4. "The Tale of __ Saltan" (Russian folk story)
5. They're sculpted in a Roman chair
6. Chicago Luvabulls, for instance
7. Give __
8. Used leverage
9. Gave away
10. Part of a playground volley
11. Designate
12. Soon
13. Take up
14. They may be crying
20. Coleridge's "Poor little foal of an oppressed race"
25. Dispenses with a tab
26. Glum
28. Academic position
29. Haunted-house supply
30. First magazine to put Steve Jobs on its cover
33. Packed, for short
34. Badgers and crows
36. Broadcast debut of 1971
37. Tug-of-war mishap
38. Italian sparkling wine
39. Quelling words
42. Run, as a gallery
43. Minority owner of ESPN
45. Apt alternative nickname to Kitty
46. "Kipling __" (2008 bio)
47. Middle name of the longest-lived vice president
48. Static
51. Hair arrangement, perhaps
52. Louis B. Mayer's boss, circa 1925
54. "No harm done"
56. Faux finish
57. Foul territory

Puzzle #85

85

ACROSS

1. Big wheel
5. Tended to leaves
10. Okra portions
14. Gramophone descendant
15. Green shade
16. Abundantly
17. Citation abbreviation
18. Mountaineer music
19. Keyed up
20. Bright red primate?
23. "Well done!"
24. Gladden
28. Free from worry
32. Heating or cooling device
35. Bidirectional, as a door
36. Judicious
37. Informal ending
38. Burning fruit?
42. Lunchbox staple
43. RSVP enclosure
44. Skip, as a syllable
45. Draw out
48. Islands near the Bahamas
49. Name meaning "born again"
50. Slip up
51. Window-shade order?
59. Source for macadamias
62. Cleared a hurdle
63. Telenovela topic
64. Out of play
65. Drink with milk
66. Green roulette bet
67. Pet parasite
68. Hotel visits
69. Former items

DOWN

1. White hat wearer
2. Edible tubes
3. Off yonder
4. Rankle
5. Title ender of the first 007 novel
6. Exclusively
7. Iconic buccaneer
8. Perpetually
9. Supermarket section
10. Jambalaya cousin
11. Former
12. Track tenaciously
13. Pen near a barn
21. Words to live by
22. Floral hoop
25. Too small to see
26. City east of South Bend
27. Obliterates
28. Silly smile
29. Qualify
30. Castle stronghold
31. Middle of the third qtr.
32. Present, as an issue
33. Rice stocked in bookstores
34. First-rate, informally
36. Small squabble
39. One of the G7 nations
40. Find out
41. '70s ring king
46. Astronomical cloud
47. Coalesce
48. Freight containers
50. Without value
52. Calamities
53. Nicely kept
54. Research material
55. Muddlement
56. Charger's choice
57. With 59 Down, detached
58. Aphrodite's boy
59. See 57 Down
60. Verizon subsidiary
61. Shading

ACROSS

1. Two-bit autocrats
8. "Let's get moving"
15. Even-tempered
16. Set to rest
17. Ranch alternative
18. Back
19. Car-wash device, for short
20. Fairly large
22. Name on NutRageous
23. Literally, "leader"
25. Pacers of yore
27. Composes
29. Buzz generator, ideally
30. Musical opening
34. Blew away, maybe
36. Positive
38. Part of Arby's logo
39. See
41. Straightens out
43. Stick-__
44. Moon of Pluto
46. Digital challenge
47. NASCAR setting
49. "Redemption" novelist
51. Some Super Bowl venues
52. Runners of experiments
55. Meeting place
56. Pickle or jam
59. Sound-stage worker
61. Step on a scale
62. Showing pique
64. Song in Jamaica Tourist Board ads
66. Rather firm
67. Halberstam subject in "The Powers That Be"
68. Tops in soreness
69. Some Mel Blanc characters

DOWN

1. One allowed to pre-board
2. Cool shade
3. End of a Groucho elephant joke
4. Campus monitors, familiarly
5. Moderately
6. Buffalo check, for one
7. Spoof
8. Flour source
9. Lifeboat supplies
10. Circular
11. Gdansk airport honoree
12. Surveys
13. __ pool
14. Action figures
21. Decliner of a 2009 Google buyout offer
24. Multiple of LII
26. Knockout
28. Takes out
31. Small, thread-like structure
32. Kicked around
33. Statement of resignation
35. They're stuck in the 60s
37. Move quickly, as a cloud
40. "Reader, I married him" speaker
42. Noodles served with soy sauce
45. Sign shorthand
48. Like "10" and "300"
50. Lakeside activity
53. Have something to declare
54. Mount topped by a mosque
56. Bombard with offers, say
57. It flattens over time
58. Kudrow's "Friends" spouse
60. Rocks, for a time
63. Appreciate
65. Fresh language

ACROSS

1. Gorillas
6. Has the rights to
10. Complain
14. Isle south of Southampton
15. Frat letters
16. Peak near Palermo
17. Ice-chest brand
18. Hang in there
19. See 23 Across
20. With 52 Across, American Museum sign that tricked visitors into leaving
22. Party hat-shaped
23. With 19 Across, radio acknowledgment
24. Pilgrim destination
26. Rambo rescuees
29. Plant's movement
31. "That's it!"
32. Laceration
33. Swiss cereal
37. With 39 Across, creator of the sign
39. See 37 Across
40. Dignified
41. Cricket field shape
42. Tax shelter, for short
43. Zodiac sign
45. Culmination
46. Oratorical skill
49. Tribulation
51. Sense of sympathy
52. See 20 Across
57. Governess of fiction
58. Far from rosy
59. Poet from Prague
60. Newcastle's river
61. One of the German Big 3
62. Cushy course
63. Source of Kremlin news
64. Secret spiller's intro
65. Wows with one-liners

DOWN

1. Airhead
2. Too expensive
3. Hybrid fruit
4. "A Christmas Carol" quartet
5. Vermont resort
6. Air France hub
7. Stuff like that
8. "It didn't work"
9. Erstwhile Atlantic crosser
10. Advocate for change
11. Make up (for)
12. About 50,000 Canadians
13. Kind of conifer
21. Sloth cousin
22. Offhand
25. Alphabetically last nation
26. Family nickname
27. Aloha Tower locale
28. Onetime Democrat rival
30. HMO workers
32. Filmed again
34. Prune slightly
35. Decoy, for instance
36. Dolby Cinema rival
38. What fills some orchards
39. Knoxville-based agcy.
41. Exotic bouquet
44. 3 Down, for instance
45. Above the ground
46. Butler of fiction
47. Slangy welcome
48. Garners
50. Bosses best humored
53. Throw off
54. Queen seen at Disneyland
55. Absolut rival
56. Abundances
58. Wide divergence

ACROSS

1. How change may come to Canadians
9. Be accommodating
15. Current danger
16. Eminent mariner of York
17. Big-12 city
18. Earn or encompass
19. Kept talking
20. False profession
22. Presents for discussion
23. Rations
24. With 28 Across, overtly abashed
25. Black O'Keeffe subject
26. Frozen-fish company co-founder
27. Matter of primary concern
28. See 24 Across
29. Steinbeck's "Mother Road"
31. Paper cutters, for short
32. Zip
33. Where some conductors work
34. 42 Down descriptor
37. Capital of Aragon
39. Wish to take back
40. Cabinet department once joined with Commerce
43. Complain softly
44. Combines
45. Mini found in Snak-Saks
46. Opposite of "okay"
47. He's left of the Dorseys on the Big Band Leaders stamps
48. They have burning desires
50. Pro athlete often linked with Wilma
51. Bugs
52. Settler along the St. Lawrence
54. Up (for)
55. Not much bread
56. Youth
57. In poor condition

DOWN

1. Scrape hard to escape
2. Loose, as a clipper
3. Pair behind the nose
4. Do-overs
5. Six Beethoven string works
6. Ian Fleming went there
7. __ house
8. Switch
9. Pinch-hit (for)
10. Fudge alternative
11. Man-cave device
12. Deja News once archived it
13. "That's what it looks like"
14. Guiding lights
21. Santalike
23. Passé roll with a hole
26. Place to land
27. Career bio
29. Have at it verbally
30. Extent
34. Interview show that got a 1993 Peabody Award
35. Public reached
36. Judge's order
37. Takes a closer look
38. Race starter, perhaps
40. Snap
41. Not generally known
42. Prefix for mania
44. Turkey part
46. Word from the Latin for "frighten"
47. Almost famous
49. Extended locks
50. Aid partner
53. First to order the Dreamliner

Puzzle #89

ACROSS

1. Roasted, in a taqueria
6. Weaken in intensity
9. Livery deliveries
14. Kick off
15. Mock-incredulous query
16. Jamaican tangelos
17. Montenegrin neighbor
18. Having major difficulty
20. With 27 and 52 Across, what a Capitol Rotunda painting depicts
22. King Hussein's queen
23. Dorm VIPs
24. Trendy boot brand
27. See 20 Across
30. Follower of brown. and rice.
32. Owneth
33. Vigorous scolding
34. Inlets, for instance
36. Equivalent of Aurora
38. Where Hungary's president lives
39. Froth-topped flow
42. Judge to be
45. Chinese zodiac beast
46. Where a copy of the painting can be seen
49. Jewelry Television rival
50. Minuscule
51. Copernicus, by birth
52. See 20 Across
57. Trumpeter, for one
60. Durance of "Smallville"
61. Less scintillating
62. Step into character
63. Fancies
64. Minuscule bits
65. "Let's do this!"
66. Ballmer who succeeded Gates

DOWN

1. Kid stuff
2. Pak of the LPGA
3. Blown away
4. Whom Woody directed to two Oscars
5. Ohio college
6. Become an expat
7. Irish rocker/philanthropist
8. '60s sessionist nation
9. Purplish Crayola color
10. "Once Upon a Time" antagonist
11. Emulating
12. Canyon edge
13. Paris-to-Lyon dir.
19. Queensland, for one
21. Crescent City, familiarly
24. Roll out
25. Snack with Dutch mustard
26. Tough key for pianists
27. Lambaste
28. Name that means "rose"
29. Scepter topper
30. Alchemist's element
31. Allurements
35. Miltie's early TV rival
37. Treacherous ones
40. Drags
41. Tundra transports
43. Poetic shade
44. Disinfectant targets
47. Room to maneuver
48. Ogle
52. News piece
53. Burn off nervous energy, maybe
54. "The __" (book on the Court)
55. Surveillance network, briefly
56. Mitigate
57. Billie Jean King Trophy org.
58. Word before tree or trick
59. Blogger's qualification

ACROSS

1. Unctuous stuff
11. Maldives is its smallest country
15. Bingbot, for one
16. Series in the DVD Martinis and Medicine Collection
17. Onetime New York home of Will Rogers
18. Tenoroon relative
19. Tape first sold in '75
20. British coronation anointment vessel
22. He directed Colin in "Total Recall"
23. Computer plug
24. Deep in the Louvre
27. Put up with a put-down
29. Primer descriptor
32. Alanis __ Morissette
36. Antithesis of love
37. Small discrepancy?
39. Built like London's Sutton House
40. Salsa ingredients?
42. Processing peaches, perhaps
44. Steak source
46. Honey, e.g.
47. Major function
50. See 8 Down
53. Subject of the 2010 documentary "Between the Folds"
54. Released, in a way
58. South Africa's "moral conscience"
59. Victim of a split decision?
61. Booster, frequently
62. Culture center
63. Highest-paid actor, per 2012 Guinness
64. Haydn masterwork

DOWN

1. Evidence-collection aid
2. Cultural fad
3. Sort of bio
4. Hexadecimal alternative
5. "Shoot"
6. They've been banned from the US since '62
7. Mars brand
8. With 50 Across, done with prime time?
9. Best friend of Charles Foster Kane
10. Literally, "citadel"
11. Excerpt from a statement
12. White fish or brown mammal
13. "Creta o Sardegna"
14. Forward
21. Theme page on HalloweenCostumes.com
23. Child development stage, per Freud
24. Battle report
25. Musical with the song "Another Pyramid"
26. Trifling
28. "Dilbert" engineer
30. Film-inspired eatery chain, familiarly
31. Common 62 Across study
33. Cat's acknowledgment
34. Something bad
35. Logical connection
38. House trailer
41. Hazard to navigation
43. Cash in a jukebox
45. Start
47. Finished work at 65, maybe
48. Not as __
49. Exhibited exhilaration
51. Name on the cover of "Fear of Fifty"
52. Aptly named duffel-bag brand
54. Options for showing percentages
55. Disney title character from Kauai
56. Top-50 boy's name, 2003-2012
57. Some Junior Leaguers
60. "King Lear" expletive

Solutions

Solution: Easy Puzzles

1

U	N	I	T	S		S	T	E	A	M		H	M	M
S	I	N	A	I		A	R	T	S	Y		O	O	O
A	L	A	R	M	C	L	O	C	K	S		U	R	L
			M	A	T	T		T	E	R	S	E		
M	A	S	T	E	R	Y		E	M	E	R	G	E	S
A	C	T	O	R	S		F	L	O	R	A	L		
S	H	O	E	S		G	L	O	R	Y		A	P	P
O	O	P	S		T	A	U	P	E		A	S	I	A
N	O	W		T	E	P	E	E		S	U	S	A	N
		A	G	R	E	E	S		S	E	R	E	N	E
A	S	T	O	U	N	D		P	A	R	A	S	O	L
P	A	C	T	S		R	O	M	P					
H	U	H		T	I	M	E	K	E	E	P	E	R	S
I	C	E		E	R	A	S	E		N	O	T	U	P
D	E	S		D	A	R	T	S		T	E	S	T	Y

2

B	A	T	H		A	B	U	T	S		C	P	A	S
A	U	R	A		L	E	T	I	N		L	A	D	Y
S	N	I	P		L	L	A	M	A		I	N	A	N
S	T	O	P	B	O	T	H	E	R	I	N	G	M	E
			Y	E	W			E	N	C				
S	L	A	N	T		B	A	D		T	H	E	F	T
H	I	H	O		D	O	G	E	A	R		T	I	E
O	N	E	W	A	Y	O	R	A	N	O	T	H	E	R
N	E	A		M	E	R	E	L	Y		A	I	L	S
E	N	D	A	T		S	E	T		A	B	C	D	E
			S	O	S			E	S	L				
W	A	L	K	O	N	E	G	G	S	H	E	L	L	S
A	C	E	S		O	V	A	L	S		T	A	U	T
T	H	A	T		R	E	V	U	E		O	K	R	A
T	Y	P	O		T	R	E	E	S		P	E	E	R

3

	M	A	G	I		T	I	P	S		I	T	E	M
S	I	R	E	S		I	D	O	L		S	W	A	Y
P	L	A	N	S		E	L	S	E		L	I	S	T
F	E	B	R	U	A	R	Y	S	E	V	E	N	T	H
			E	E	L		E	V	E					
T	S	K		S	O	B		E	R	R	A	T	A	
O	H	O		O	U	S	T		S	O	N	I	C	
M	A	R	C	H	F	O	U	R	T	E	E	N	T	H
E	L	E	N	A		Y	E	A	R		O	L	E	
S	T	A	N	Z	A		P	U	P		Y	E	S	
			E	T	C		S	I	P					
A	P	R	I	L	E	I	G	H	T	E	E	N	T	H
L	A	I	R		A	R	E	A		C	A	I	R	O
A	L	S	O		S	C	A	M		E	R	N	I	E
S	E	E	N		E	A	R	S		S	L	A	M	

4

W	E	D	S		A	R	T	S		S	L	E	E	P
A	V	O	N		P	O	R	T		W	E	A	V	E
I	O	W	A		R	O	A	R		A	T	S	E	A
S	K	E	I	N	O	F	Y	A	R	N		E	R	R
T	E	L	L	O	N		S	W	E	E	T			
			I	S	M			L	E	A	S	E	D	
A	W	M	A	N		O	M	N	I		P	L	E	A
C	H	E	C	K	I	N	G	A	C	C	O	U	N	T
L	O	S	T		R	O	M	P		O	N	R	Y	E
U	S	A	U	S	A		E	R	A					
			P	A	T	S	Y		E	L	I	C	I	T
W	A	S		S	E	C	O	N	D	S	T	O	R	Y
I	R	I	S	H		O	D	O	R		S	L	O	P
S	A	L	S	A		F	E	T	A		N	O	N	E
E	B	O	N	Y		F	L	E	W		O	R	S	O

5

C	O	M	P		C	O	N	D	O		G	R	A	B
O	P	A	L		A	V	O	I	D		R	O	M	E
M	E	R	E		R	A	V	E	D		A	P	E	S
B	R	E	A	D	P	L	A	T	E		V	E	N	T
	A	S	T	R	O			S	P	Y				
		S	O	B		S	T	U	B	B	E	D		
S	H	A	W		L	O	A	N		B	O	A	R	D
T	A	X	I		S	O	N	I	C		A	S	I	A
A	R	E	N	T		M	Y	T	H		T	H	E	Y
R	E	D	E	E	M	S		S	E	A				
			G	E	E			C	R	E	D	O		
W	O	O	L		S	T	E	A	K	K	N	I	F	E
A	R	I	A		H	E	D	G	E		D	A	T	A
V	A	N	S		E	A	G	E	R		O	N	E	S
E	L	K	S		D	R	E	S	S		W	A	N	T

6

P	A	S	S		T	E	N		C	L	A	D
A	C	H	E		E	A	U		V	E	X	E	S
T	H	A	W		A	T	M		S	A	L	S	A
C	O	R	N	C	R	I	B		K	E	P	T
H	O	P		R	U	N		H	E	Y		E	S	S
		P	E	P		P	O	P			R	T	E
S	P	A	R	E		B	A	S	I	C		A	I	L
T	E	L	E	P	H	O	N	E	C	R	A	D	L	E
A	R	T		S	O	R	T	S		I	D	O	L	S
I	I	I		H	E	S			S	T	S
R	O	T		S	O	D		A	L	I		A	H	A
	D	U	S	T			T	R	U	C	K	B	E	D
I	D	E	A	S		R	I	M		H	A	R	E
C	E	L	L	O		E	S	P		A	T	O	P
S	L	E	W		X	E	S		N	E	S	T

7

```
A S P E N   S P R Y     A W E
S I E G E   P R I O R   L I D
O R E O S   L I N G O   O R E
F I R S T A I D K I T   H E N
      L I T E     I P A D S
  P A P E R S   A N N A
C E L L   T R A I L M I X
A R E A   J E R K Y   A O N E
B U G S P R A Y     C O N S
    M A S T   L A G E R S
P U M A S   H A L E
U S E   S L E E P I N G B A G
F U R   E A R N S   I N A N E
F A R   S W I N E   E A S E L
S L Y   S E A S   S T E W S
```

8

```
W E S T   S L U M P   A N T E
R U L E   T O N E R   B E A M
A R I A   A N I S E   H A L T
P O P P I N G T H E C O R K
      O D D     N O R
H A I T I   M A G   D R A F T
O L D   O P E N U P   E L L A
S L A M M I N G T H E D O O R
T O R E   G O E S I N   O A R
S T E E L   T R Y   S O F T Y
      K E G     O U R
B A N G I N G T H E D R U M
R A V E   R E L A Y   E A S E
I R I S   T R I C E   A C E S
B E D S   H O B O S   L E S S
```

9

```
A S K S   D O R A   A C O R N
S H O T   U K E S   R A D I O
H A R E   F L A P   G R O S S
E V E R   F A M I L Y T R E E
S E A N C E   S E A L
    O L D   T E A B A G
A S T I R   R E S T   C O L A
S N A K E I N T H E G R A S S
P I P E   S O S O   A E S O P
S T E A L S     P A L
    O U T S   B A A B A A
G E O R G E B U S H   B A N G
P A R E S   O R T O   E T T E
A R E N O   N E A R   T H I N
S P O O N   E R R S   S E C T
```

10

```
P U R R S   B A T S   W A R S
I S A A C   A B E T   I D O L
N E R V E   R O A R   N O V A
G R E E N H O U S E   D R E W
      T E N T   E A S E D
B R O W S E   I T C H
A U D I   D E A N   T I A R A
I S O N   S N I T S   E L I S
T H R E W   D R O P   L O B S
    B A R S   E L D E S T
A B O D E   M A N E
T R O T   C H A N D E L I E R
H U R T   E A S T   W O R D Y
A B E L   S H O E   A D A G E
W A D E   S A N D   Y E S E S
```

11

```
S T A F F   S T E P   C R A B
H O T E L   T O T E   H E M I
A G I L E   A U T O   E V E N
M A P L E S Y R U P   R U N G
      C O S   L A R E D O
  S A F E R   C H E W Y
A N T I   T R U E   O C T E T
S I N G S   A P R   L O O M S
S T O N E   V I S A   L A M P
    E A S E D   R E A D Y
S H O W M E     S I N
H I L T   A V O C A D O D I P
U P D O   L O B E   E R A S E
S P I N   A T O N   A S Y E T
H O E S   B E E T   R O S E S
```

12

```
B E E R S   B A L L   L A C K
L A P E L   A R I A   A L A N
A S I D E   T E E N   S O M E
S E C O N D H A N D   T H E E
T D S   D O E S   S M A L L
    D E N S   C C I
I M P A R T   T R A I N E E S
N A R Y   L A I T Y   U T A H
A D O P T I O N   E S T A T E
    L E E K   A N T E
R E L A X   A N N A   F C C
I R A N   D I N N E R H O U R
T O R N   U S D A   T O R T E
E D G E   C T R L   L A C E S
S E E R   T O E S   E X E R T
```

Solution: Easy Puzzles

13

SAGE / BOCA / BARS
DIVAN / IRAS / ARIA
INERT / RELY / REDS
BARBIEDOLL / BASS
SIT / RRS / SURE
BEING / MORSEL
HAHA / NERD / SPADE
APART / SEE / YOKES
VERGE / TEAM / LENS
EXPAND / KNIFE
ITES / SNO / KOS
TEEN / BARLEYSOUP
ARAB / ALAI / ELATE
SISI / TSPS / RILED
KEEN / EAST / STAR

14

BUILT / CAMP / BETS
OPRAH / ARIA / RARE
STATE / PINS / AREA
COSTUMEDESIGNER
ESE / DEN
USH / ALSO / SUREST
NCAA / OILS / SINCE
CASTINGDIRECTOR
ALTOS / HERE / HELM
PEOPLE / REFS / RDS
ALE / ETS
CINEMATOGRAPHER
OREO / TUNE / CRIME
MORN / EDEN / KEVIN
ENDS / SEAT / SEETO

15

MIL / BILLS / ACME
AIDE / ADIOS / THIN
PLEA / WEAVE / HAND
ROADFLARE / BENDS
FEELS / SAND
AFFORD / PASSES
MELON / HAILS / LAW
FEAT / BURNT / DIVA
MDS / DANCE / BREED
SHRINK / COARSE
LEND / ALLOW
SLIDE / FLOORLAMP
TAGS / MAIDS / OREO
ACHE / ADAGE / TENT
BETA / RESET / SAD

16

SLAP / THROW / ISLE
EURO / HEIDI / SCAM
EATS / RATON / WRIT
DUSTCOVER / FEUDS
PLAYS / SLAB
SAWOUT / LEARNER
PLANE / FAINT / UFO
ELSE / TIRED / GRIP
NAH / OINKS / AISLE
THANKED / AGREES
SEER / CAMEL
ACHED / POLISHOFF
CLOD / RABID / OGLE
TORE / ACRES / ORES
SPED / MEANT / DEES

17

SIRS / METE / FLAW
BISON / ODOR / LACE
IGLOO / PERU / EVER
ONEMOMENTPLEASE
SPA / ETA
BLT / SKIES / NESTS
YEWS / ERA / ACTIII
WAITJUSTASECOND
ASLEEP / INC / HUGE
YELPS / ENTER / XED
SAD / NET
ILLBERIGHTTHERE
DOOR / OSLO / IRATE
OBOE / SOAP / NOVEL
LEND / ENDS / AWES

18

WOVE / WASAT / SPEW
ARIA / ALONE / HERE
LEER / TORTE / HARE
TOWNMEETING / COD
ORS / ALTERS
SAFETY / RIGOR
OHARE / RACE / AMIS
LOCALGOVERNMENT
DYES / ODES / OPTIN
ESSES / ASSETS
GRADES / ORE
ROD / CIVICCENTER
AGOG / PATCH / EASE
SURE / ENSUE / AMPS
SEEM / DEARS / TENT

Solution: Easy Puzzles

Solution: Easy Puzzles

19

```
C O T . . S P R E E . S H O T
R A G S . T R I E S . L E N O
O H I O . A I S L E . E L M S
C U F F L I N K S . P I P E S
. . T A R T S . L A G . . .
P O P E S . M I S H A P S . .
O U R S . T A P I N S . L E A
K N I T T I N G N E E D L E S
E C O . O B T A I N . E O N S
D E R I D E S . P A T S Y . .
. . R A T . T O W E L . . . .
D E C O Y . W A T E R S K I S
I C O N . S A N T A . T I R E
S H O E . T I G E R . O D I E
H O L D . S T O R Y . S S N
```

20

```
T I A R A . S L A M . S H O T
G O B A D . P I T A . O O Z E
I W I S H . A M O K . U P O N
F A T H E R T I M E . L E N D
. . R E S T . M A S S E S . .
P R O B E S . D E L I . . . .
S E M I . E M M Y . I S L A M
S A N G . T I B E T . T A C O
T R I B E . N A S A . E C H O
. R E A D . S P R E E S . . .
C A V O R T . S I T E . . . .
S L I T . M O T H E R L O D E
P O S H . O R E O . K A P O W
A N T E . S E E P . U N T I E
N E A R . T S P S . P E S T S
```

21

```
S N A P S . S I L T . A W L S
H O V E L . A M I D . V I A L
A T O N E . J A M S . I N T O
W I N N E B A G O . Y A C H T
. . A P O K E . B A T H E S .
L A W M E N . P U R E E . . .
I C I E R . A D O R N . S O W
S I N . A C O R N . T I E . .
A D D . T W E E T . A G E N T
. O R E O S . C L E R K S . .
O H W E L L . F A U L T . . .
P A P A L . W I N T E R I Z E
E R A S . G E N T . G E N O A
R E N O . O R E S . E A R N S
A M E N . V E R Y . S L E E T
```

22

```
S P A S . S T A L E . R A I D
A R C H . L E M O N . E L S E
S I T E . A N I S E . C O L A
E M I L Y P O S T . H O T E L
. . T E A R S . D I M . . . .
B A S E S T . L I P B A L M .
O V E R . C L A S P . M A I .
N E W S P A P E R C O L U M N
E R E . S T A I D . I S E E .
S T R E A M S . B A L E R S .
. . E L S . D A I S Y . . . .
A L A R M . N O R T H P O L E
S E M I . L E G I T . A R E A
T A M E . P O I S E . D E A R
O D O R . S N E E R . S O N S
```

23

```
A N G S T . T E A R . N I T E
T O R T E . A X L E . A R A B
T R I A L . B E E T . G A L A
S I N G L E O C C U P A N C Y
. . . S N O . R A T . . . . .
S A L S A S . T E N T . H E Y
A V A I L . P E S T . E V E .
D O U B L E E X P O S U R E S
L I D . X R A Y . A S O N E .
Y D S . A T M S . B L A S T S
. . A I R . P I E . . . . . .
T R I P L E W O R D S C O R E
A U R A . M A X I . M O W E R
R E A R . E V E N . A R E N A
P S S T . S E N T . N E S T S
```

24

```
M E S A . A C E S . I N T O W
O P A L . T H A W . S E I N E
M I S S . D O R A . W I N C E
S C H O L A R L Y . E G G E D
. . E W E S . N A H . . . . .
G A R D E N . G A R B A G E .
A S A I R . S L A P . O R O N
S K I S . S P E W S . R I O T
P E S O . T E A K . B L A S E
S W E R V E D . G E Y S E R .
. . D E W . N C A A . . . . .
A M B E R . L E I S U R E L Y
N E A R S . O A T H . A R E A
T A B L E . A T E E . P I N K
S T A Y S . N O D S . S E T S
```

Solution: Easy Puzzles

25

```
C P O S ▪ S C A L E ▪ A C E D
R A P T ▪ E L L I S ▪ R A T E
O R E O ▪ T A L E S ▪ C R A M
C A R N A T I O N ▪ P A B L O
▪ ▪ E N E M Y ▪ J U D O ▪ ▪
V A C A T E ▪ P A R E N S ▪
A D A G E ▪ C R I M E ▪ A T E
T I R E ▪ C O I N S ▪ S T E M
S O D ▪ C A N O E ▪ S T E A M
▪ S I T U P S ▪ H A R D L Y
▪ O A T S ▪ S T A K E ▪ ▪
P O L L S ▪ C A R P E N T E R
S H O O ▪ P A Y U P ▪ G O R E
S I G N ▪ T R A C E ▪ T R I P
T O Y S ▪ A S H E N ▪ H O E S
```

26

```
L A N D ▪ R A B B I ▪ S W A M
I C E R ▪ E L L E N ▪ T A L E
P L E A ▪ D I A N A ▪ A T I T
S U R F B O A R D ▪ S T E V E
▪ ▪ T E N S E ▪ S O U R E D ▪
U P S I D E ▪ R E N E W ▪ ▪
C L A N S ▪ D I E T ▪ I G O
L O N G ▪ H A N D S ▪ S N O W
A D D ▪ D I R K S ▪ L E G A L
▪ B R I N E ▪ R O A S T S
F L U E N T ▪ E R E C T
L A C E S ▪ B E A C H B A L L
A S K S ▪ M A R G E ▪ E R I E
I S E E ▪ P R I E D ▪ L I E S
R O T S ▪ G E E S E ▪ T A N S
```

27

```
T R O T ▪ S C A R ▪ S T R O P
N A S A ▪ P O S E ▪ E R O D E
T I L L ▪ R U I N ▪ E A T I N
D O C T O R S O F F I C E ▪
▪ ▪ H U T ▪ O I L ▪ ▪
C U T S I T ▪ P A R T ▪ O F F
A S H E N ▪ B U R G ▪ G U R U
C H E C K O U T C O U N T E R
T E S T ▪ C O T S ▪ B A G E L
I R E ▪ B A Y S ▪ M O T O R S
▪ A O L ▪ S E A ▪
S U B W A Y S T A T I O N
C A N A L ▪ I P A D ▪ S P E W
A N I S E ▪ P O L O ▪ L A T E
D E T E R ▪ S T E W ▪ E L S E
```

28

```
G O A D S ▪ S A P S ▪ S P A M
O P T I C ▪ H U L A ▪ C O P E
L E T G O ▪ O R A L ▪ A L E S
F R Y I N G P A N S ▪ T O S S
▪ T E A ▪ S A L T ▪ ▪
P A Y S ▪ T A B ▪ S E E T H E
A V E ▪ R O S E S ▪ G R A Y S
C A S S E R O L E D I S H E S
K N O L L ▪ F L E E T ▪ O N E
S T R E A M ▪ E S P ▪ S E A S
▪ E X E C ▪ T H E ▪
B O O K ▪ D U T C H O V E N S
E R I E ▪ A R E A ▪ T E P E E
E E L S ▪ L I E S ▪ E R E C T
P O S T ▪ S O M E ▪ L E E K S
```

29

```
S P O T ▪ G E M S ▪ C R U S T
L A V A ▪ O D I E ▪ R A N T O
O P A L ▪ V I L E ▪ A D D U P
W A L L D E C O R A T I O N S
▪ A R T ▪ T E A ▪
C R A M I N ▪ D E S ▪ L O A N
A U R A S ▪ S A G E S ▪ O R E
C L O S E T O R G A N I Z E R
H E M ▪ S H O E S ▪ O N E N D
E R A S ▪ I T S ▪ M O N D A Y
▪ C N N ▪ P U P ▪
V I D E O G A M E S Y S T E M
I R A N I ▪ M A P S ▪ H I D E
S O R T S ▪ E L S E ▪ I R I S
A N T S Y ▪ N E I L ▪ P E T S
```

30

```
G N A T S ▪ S P A R ▪ P I N S
R I V E T ▪ C I T E ▪ I D E A
O N I C E ▪ A L O T ▪ C L A P
W A S H A B L E M A R K E R S
▪ D I D ▪ I V Y ▪
P O E T I C ▪ P A L S ▪ A T M
O H A R E ▪ M A T E ▪ G L U E
W A T E R C O L O R P A I N T
E R I E ▪ R A M P ▪ E M C E E
R A N ▪ C U T S ▪ S T E E D S
▪ A I M ▪ S I N ▪
E R A S A B L E C R A Y O N S
L A C K ▪ L U R E ▪ M A R I E
M I M E ▪ E A R N ▪ E L A T E
S L E D ▪ D U S T ▪ S E L E S
```

Solution: Easy Puzzles

31

```
C A B S   G O A L   B O A T S
A N E W   I D L E   A R E A S
N I L E   N O V A   R E R U N
I S L E   G R A S S R O O T S
T E E T H E     T H E
      E R R S   I D O T O O
T O N E R   A A R P   A R O W
I V Y L E A G U E S C H O O L
M A P S   T E N D   A U T O S
E L D E S T   A S A P
      H I S   S E N S E S
P E A J A C K E T S   O P E N
A C T U P   U R G E   T I R E
S H A D E   L O I N   E R I E
T O D O S   L O F T   S E E R
```

32

```
S H A M   W A D E R   R A M P
P I N A   A S O R E   E R I E
E G G S   R I L E D   L I N T
C H E S S M A T C H   A D D S
    C R E P E   T O N Y
        A S S T   T A R T A N
S N A P   T A R T   S A U C E
P I V O T   S I R   A C R E S
A L I K E   S E E R   E N D S
R E S E L L   D E E R
      R E A D   C E D A R
S H A G   P R I Z E F I G H T
T U B A   C O R E D   V I E W
A L U M   A N I S E   A L T O
G A T E   T E S T S   S E T S
```

33

```
S C A L P   T S P S   B L T S
T O W E L   A T I T   R I O T
A R E N A   M O N A   O N T O
R E D S N A P P E R   W E A R
      E R A S   C A N D L E
D E P O T S   S H A G
O D O R   O R E O   A R G U E
N I N A   N A S A L   A L K A
S T E N O   P E K E   V E E S
    G U S T   D R Y E S T
C A M E R A   F A T E
A S A P   Y E L L O W C O R N
T I R E   I T A L   O L D I E
E D G E   N A M E   R A I D S
R E E L   G L E N   K N E E S
```

34

```
M A Y O   S P E W   S C R A P
A L E S   A L T O   C O I N S
M E A L   M U C K   O U S T S
A C R O S S T H E S T R E E T
      C O O   I T S
S C R E E N   L A D   E M U S
A L I E N   E A S E S   I N K
W A L K I N G D I S T A N C E
I R E   C O O L S   E X I L E
N A Y S   S S E   P R E S E T
    P I E   T O E
A R O U N D T H E C O R N E R
H A D N T   R A N K   A U T O
E V O K E   A L O E   G L A D
M E R Y L   P O R T   E L S E
```

35

```
S P O T   P R O M S   E P I C
L A V A   H U R O N   L A N E
A P E S   O N E A L   P R O S
P A R T I T I O N   H A D N T
    I C O N S   P E S O
T E P E E S   B E L O N G S
A M A S S   S P I E D   A L L
C A R T   S P O O L   O B O E
O I L   S E E D S   P U L S E
S L I P P E D   D E T E S T
    A L U M   S T E A L
N O M A D   P A R T R I D G E
E D E N   C U T I E   N O E L
W I N E   D R I E R   E R R S
S E T S   S E N D S   S A M E
```

36

```
P A S S   M I A M I   A C M E
A L O T   A N T I C   F L A W
I S L E   S O O T Y   F O R E
D O O R C H I M E   D E C K S
    N O E L S   S O C K
W I D E N S   T O S T A D A
A M I S S   A D O R E   L E I
I S N T   S C O R E   C A L L
T E N   S A R G E   C A R V E
S T E R I L E   F O R M E D
    R E N T   R E I G N
R O B E S   F I R E S I R E N
A B E L   E A V E S   V I L E
S O L E   T R A C T   A T M S
H E L D   D E L T A   L E S S
```

Solution: Easy Puzzles

37

W	A	N	T		A	T	M	S		A	L	S	O
B	E	L	O	W		T	R	E	E		R	E	A	P
U	N	D	U	E		T	U	N	E		M	A	L	E
S	T	A	N	L	E	Y	C	U	P		O	V	E	N
			V	A	S	E			P	R	E	S	S
S	H	A	R	E	S			A	H	O	Y
I	O	W	A		E	F	I	L	E	S		U	S	O
T	H	E	M	E	D	A	L	O	F	H	O	N	O	R
S	O	S		G	I	M	L	E	T		I	D	L	E
		C	O	N	E			I	G	L	O	O	S
A	T	L	A	S			A	B	E	L
B	E	A	R		B	L	U	E	R	I	B	B	O	N
A	N	T	E		L	I	D	S		T	A	L	O	N
T	O	E	S		O	M	I	T		C	R	E	P	E
E	R	R	S		B	O	O	S		H	E	W	S

38

	H	G	T	S		P	A	R	E		A	S	P	S
M	A	R	I	E		U	S	E	S		C	H	A	T
P	L	A	N	T		R	S	V	P		C	O	P	E
H	O	M	E	F	R	I	E	S		S	T	R	A	W
			R	A	F	T			A	N	T
S	O	C	I	E	T	Y		O	P	P	O	S	E	S
C	L	O	V	E	R		P	A	L	S		T	S	P
I	D	L	E		A	O	R	T	A		D	A	T	A
F	E	D		A	C	R	E		S	A	U	C	E	R
I	N	C	A	G	E	S		S	T	R	O	K	E	S
		E	S	T			M	A	I	M
M	A	R	K	S		H	O	T	C	O	F	F	E	E
O	R	E	O		Z	I	T	I		R	I	O	T	S
B	E	A	U		E	V	E	N		E	D	I	T	S
S	A	L	T		E	E	L	S		D	O	L	E

39

	M	O	N	O		G	O	N	E		P	A	L	S
G	I	V	E	N		I	C	E	S		A	R	I	A
A	L	E	R	T		Z	E	S	T		N	E	O	N
P	A	N	O	R	A	M	A	S		T	H	A	N	K
E	N	S		I	N	O	N		S	R	A
		P	A	T	S			D	A	U	N	T	S
I	N	H	A	L	E		D	O	N	E	D	E	A	L
K	E	E	N		L	A	C	E	D		L	A	K	E
E	X	I	T	P	O	L	L		D	E	E	M	E	D
	T	R	O	U	P	E		R	U	N	S
		M	M	E		F	A	N	G		A	S	S
S	T	R	I	P		P	A	N	E	L	I	S	T	S
L	O	O	M		S	A	L	K		A	D	M	A	N
A	N	T	E		E	L	S	E		N	E	A	R	S
B	E	E	S		W	E	E	D		D	A	D	S

40

R	A	F	T	S		H	A	H	A		O	P	E	C
O	P	E	R	A		E	T	A	L		B	O	R	E
M	E	T	A	L		L	O	L	L		A	L	A	N
A	D	A	M	S	A	P	P	L	E		M	A	S	T
			A	M	S			G	L	A	R	E	S
C	O	A	R	S	E		F	L	E	E
O	K	G	O		S	K	I	P		F	L	E	A	S
P	R	O	P	O	S	I	N	G	A	T	O	A	S	T
E	A	G	E	R		L	E	A	S		B	R	I	E
			S	E	T	S		P	R	E	L	A	W
P	E	S	T	O	S			L	E	O
R	A	T	E		C	A	S	I	N	O	C	H	I	P
O	G	R	E		O	X	E	N		S	H	A	D	E
P	L	A	N		R	E	E	K		T	A	T	E	R
S	E	W	S		T	S	K	S		S	T	E	A	K

41

C	L	A	S	H		G	Y	N	T		J	I	B	S
P	E	S	T	O		N	O	A	H		A	Q	U	A
O	N	T	A	P		A	U	T	O		B	U	N	S
S	T	O	R	E	O	W	N	E	R	S		I	T	S
			S	N	A	G			P	A	T	S	Y
B	I	G	F	O	O	T		S	P	O	T
A	R	E	A			T	H	R	O	W	R	U	G
B	A	L	T	I	M	O	R	E	O	R	I	O	L	E
A	N	T	I	M	O	N	Y			L	U	N	A
		M	A	D	E		C	O	A	L	T	A	R
S	C	R	A	G		A	S	H	E
Q	U	A		O	F	F	S	H	O	R	E	O	I	L
U	R	I	S		O	R	C	A		I	M	A	G	E
A	S	T	I		P	A	I	R		A	M	T	O	O
B	E	T	S		S	N	I	P		L	A	S	T	S

42

C	A	R	A	T		P	E	A	R		B	R	A	Y
E	L	A	T	E		E	M	M	A		R	A	G	E
A	L	P	H	A		S	A	I	D		A	M	E	N
S	U	P	E	R	S	T	I	T	I	O	N
E	D	E	N		H	O	L	E	U	P		M	B	A
S	E	D	A	T	E			S	T	R	E	A	M
			U	B	O	A	T			A	N	D	Y
	U	R	B	A	N	L	E	G	E	N	D
N	I	N	A			E	P	E	E	S
E	D	I	T	O	R			E	P	O	C	H	S
T	O	T		W	E	A	V	E	S		C	H	A	T
	O	L	D	W	I	V	E	S	T	A	L	E
Z	I	T	I		C	A	G	E		P	A	S	T	E
I	C	O	N		A	K	I	N		E	N	T	E	R
P	E	E	K		P	E	L	T		W	E	E	D	S

Solution: Easy Puzzles

43

M	A	M	A		S	I	S	S	Y		R	O	B	S
E	P	I	C		A	T	O	N	E		O	R	E	O
G	U	S	T	A	V	E	F	L	A	U	B	E	R	T
		C	I	N	E	M	A		N	E	I	G	H	
B	A	H		T	A	S		P	G	A		D	E	A
A	L	I	B	I	S		P	R	O	B		A	N	T
D	I	E	U			F	R	I	L	L	S			
		F	L	O	Z	I	E	G	F	E	L	D		
		B	U	E	N	O	S			O	W	E	S	
P	O	T		T	R	A	P		M	O	B	I	L	E
I	C	U		L	O	L		B	O	G		N	I	X
A	T	R	I	A			P	U	T	R	I	D		
G	O	E	S	W	I	T	H	T	H	E	F	L	O	W
E	P	E	E		S	M	I	T	E		S	E	R	A
T	I	N	E		M	I	L	E	R		O	D	E	S

44

B	E	L	L	S		T	R	A	P		S	W	A	P
A	T	E	A	T		E	U	R	O		H	O	S	E
C	R	E	M	E		S	L	I	P		A	R	T	S
H	E	R	B	A	L	T	E	A	S		S	K	I	T
			M	A	Y		T	A	T	E	R	S		
R	A	F	T	E	D		A	V	A	T	A	R		
A	C	R	I	D		S	C	A	R	F		B	R	A
S	H	O	P		D	A	R	N	S		T	E	A	R
P	E	Z		L	E	V	E	E		P	I	E	C	E
		E	L	A	T	E	S		A	L	A	S	K	A
M	A	N	A	G	E			S	P	A				
A	S	P	S		C	H	O	P	P	Y	S	E	A	S
S	T	E	T		T	A	P	E		A	U	D	I	O
O	R	A	L		E	L	A	L		C	R	E	D	O
N	O	S	Y		D	E	L	L		T	E	N	E	T

45

S	A	S	S		W	A	W	A		A	C	I	D	S
K	N	I	T		A	T	O	P		R	O	N	D	O
I	T	S	A	N	Y	O	N	E	S	G	U	E	S	S
			C	A	L	M		S	H	O	P			
A	C	A	C	I	A	S		U	T	O	P	I	A	
R	O	T	A	R	Y		L	I	T		N	E	R	D
P	L	A	T	O		I	O	N	I	C		R	K	O
		N	O	B	O	D	Y	K	N	O	W	S		
E	W	E		I	D	E	A	S		S	H	O	E	D
R	E	N	D		D	S	L		S	T	I	N	T	S
R	E	D	E	E	M		C	O	N	T	A	C	T	
		I	R	A	S		A	B	E	E				
Y	O	U	C	A	N	N	E	V	E	R	T	E	L	L
E	A	S	E	S		O	V	E	R		I	S	E	E
T	R	A	D	E		B	E	D	S		E	T	A	T

46

T	R	E	A	D		P	A	C	K	S		A	C	E
B	O	W	I	E		A	L	O	N	E		S	I	X
S	P	E	L	L	I	N	G	B	E	E		S	R	I
P	E	R	S	U	A	D	E		E	F	F	E	C	T
				S	M	A	R	T		I	O	T	A	S
C	A	P	R	I			I	R	A	T	E			
I	D	A	H	O		M	A	I	L		A	P	E	
T	O	R	O	N	T	O		B	L	U	E	J	A	Y
E	S	T			E	D	G	E		S	C	A	L	E
		L	A	X	E	R			D	O	R	M	S	
S	T	E	A	L		L	O	T	T	O				
C	A	N	D	I	D		C	A	R	L	O	A	D	S
O	P	T		B	A	S	E	B	A	L	L	B	A	T
O	E	R		I	N	T	R	O		A	D	E	L	E
P	R	Y		S	A	Y	S	O		R	E	L	I	T

47

R	A	T		D	A	G		A	K	C		C	O	W
E	V	E		E	R	R		U	N	O		A	H	A
D	I	E		B	R	I	S	T	O	L		S	I	R
C	A	T		T	O	P	T	O	B	O	T	T	O	M
A	T	O	Z		W	E	E		R	U	R	A	L	
R	O	T	O	R	S		M	R	S		B	O	N	Y
D	R	A	N	O		S	T	A	R	E				
		L	E	F	T	T	O	R	I	G	H	T		
		L	O	O	S	E		G	O	A	T	S		
C	O	R	Y		O	P	T		A	S	P	I	R	E
A	R	E	A	S		E	R	N		S	L	I	M	
B	A	C	K	T	O	F	R	O	N	T		O	B	I
A	T	E		A	V	E	N	G	E	R		R	U	N
N	O	D		M	E	T		U	A	E		E	T	A
A	R	E		P	R	E		E	L	K		D	E	L

48

B	O	D	E		R	A	P	S		B	E	T	O	N
O	P	U	S		E	D	I	T		A	T	O	N	E
C	A	S	T	A	V	O	T	E		T	A	S	T	E
A	L	K	A	L	I		T	A	C	T		S	O	D
			T	E	L	L		M	A	L	T	A		
		H	E	R	E	O	F		R	E	A	S	O	N
A	P	E		T	R	O	O	P		S	P	A	D	E
B	E	A	K			P	A	L			S	L	O	W
C	A	V	E	S		S	L	A	P	S		A	R	T
S	L	E	E	P	S			S	T	A	T	E	D	
			A	P	A	R	T		E	R	R	S		
C	B	S		T	I	E	S		D	E	C	A	D	E
A	L	I	S	T		T	H	R	O	W	A	F	I	T
R	O	G	U	E		R	A	I	N		P	R	O	D
E	T	H	E	R		A	D	D	S		E	O	N	S

Solution: Easy + Medium Puzzles

49

N	O	D	S		A	N	I	M	E		O	G	R	E
A	R	I	A		M	O	R	A	L		P	L	E	A
S	E	P	I	A	P	H	O	T	O		E	A	S	T
C	I	N	D	Y		E	N	S	I	G	N	S		
A	D	E		E	L	L	E		L	I	S	L	E	
R	A	T	S		A	P	R	I	C	O	T	J	A	M
		I	B	M		S	N	O	B		A	R	M	
F	O	R	R	E	A	L		T	H	A	T	W	A	Y
U	P	I		D	R	E	W		O	L	E			
J	U	N	K	D	R	A	W	E	R		A	C	T	S
I	S	S	U	E		I	N	T	O		L	I	T	
	E	N	D	E	M	I	C		T	N	O	T	E	
G	R	O	G		N	O	V	A	S	C	O	T	I	A
M	I	F	F		O	M	E	G	A		S	H	A	M
T	O	F	U		S	A	T	E	D		H	E	N	S

50

B	A	R	K		S	P	A	R		U	P	T	O
A	L	A	I		M	A	R	I	E		T	E	E	N
S	A	Y	T	H	E	W	O	R	D		T	E	A	L
I	M	O		O	R	E	S		C	H	E	R	R	Y
N	O	N	S	K	I	D		C	H	A	R			
		P	E	T		C	L	I	M	A	X	E	S	
A	B	B	E	Y		T	H	A	N		S	E	A	T
P	L	E	A		D	R	A	M	A		O	R	C	A
B	U	L	K		R	A	S	P		B	U	S	H	Y
S	E	L	F	M	A	D	E		B	A	N			
		R	A	G	E		D	R	Y	D	O	C	K	
T	W	E	E	T	S		C	I	A	O		N	R	A
H	O	L	E		T	A	L	K	T	U	R	K	E	Y
O	V	A	L		E	P	E	E	S		D	E	M	O
R	E	L	Y		R	E	F	S		A	Y	E	S	

51

H	O	R	T	O	N		I	M	A	C		P	B	J
A	V	E	E	N	O		N	Y	S	E		R	E	C
H	A	M	L	E	T		C	D	P	L	A	Y	E	R
	A	L	T		L	A	O	S		C	O	N	E	
J	K	R	O	W	L	I	N	G		S	H	R	E	W
A	I	R	F	O	I	L		S	K	Y				
D	O	I		T	A	H	I	T	I		E	A	T	
E	W	E		Q	R	C	O	D	E	S		P	R	O
D	A	D		T	E	S	T	E	R		I	T	O	
		H	I	S		A	N	I	S	T	O	N		
S	I	T	U	P		U	V	T	A	T	T	O	O	S
I	D	O	L		E	P	E	E		G	Y	M		
X	Y	P	L	A	N	E	S		S	I	M	I	L	E
E	L	S		H	I	N	T		P	R	I	Z	E	S
S	L	Y		A	D	D	S		F	L	E	E	T	S

52

H	O	P	E		T	E	E	S		I	N	F	E	R
E	V	I	L		O	G	R	E		N	O	L	T	E
R	E	A	D	I	N	G	R	A	I	L	R	O	A	D
O	R	N	E	R	Y		H	O	E		O	T	S	
S	T	O	R	K		P	L	A	N	T	E	R		
				S	T	O	W	S		M	A	C		
B	O	A	R	D	W	A	L	K		S	A	R	I	S
K	A	B	O	O	M		T	A	L	E	N	T		
S	T	A	L	E		P	A	R	K	P	L	A	C	E
	S	T	L		P	A	T	I	O					
	R	E	S	C	A	P	E	D		A	P	A	R	T
R	A	M		A	I	R		T	R	A	D	E	R	
E	L	E	C	T	R	I	C	C	O	M	P	A	N	Y
D	O	N	E	E		K	E	E	N		A	P	E	S
O	T	T	E	R		A	L	O	E		S	T	E	T

53

S	O	F	T		M	A	M	A	S		S	T	I	R
A	L	I	A		O	D	D	L	Y		A	W	A	Y
F	I	F	T	Y	S	E	V	E	N		M	E	G	A
E	V	E		E	L	N	I	N	O		I	N	O	N
R	E	S	A	L	E		E	N	D	A	T			
		F	L	Y	I	N		Y	U	M	Y	U	M	
M	E	S	A	S		N	O	T	M	E		O	S	U
E	M	I	R		I	O	T	A	S		S	N	A	G
M	I	X		U	N	W	E	D		D	O	E	R	S
O	T	T	E	R	S		S	A	H	I	B			
		Y	A	L	I	E		A	C	A	D	I	A	
P	F	F	T		S	T	A	B	L	E		E	K	G
A	L	O	E		T	H	I	R	T	Y	N	I	N	E
P	O	U	R		E	E	R	I	E		I	C	O	N
A	W	R	Y		D	R	Y	E	R		N	E	W	T

54

M	E	L	T	S		C	L	A	R	A		L	A	B
E	L	I	O	T		O	I	L	E	R		O	R	E
L	I	T	M	U	S	P	A	P	E	R		U	S	A
			D	E	E	R		L	E	N	N	O	N	
H	E	L	M	E	T	S			S	I	G	N	S	
O	N	I	O	N	S		S	U	B	T	L	E		
A	V	E	R	T		C	A	R	E	S		C	H	E
R	O	D	E		J	A	U	N	T		A	H	E	M
D	Y	E		B	E	S	T	S		P	L	A	N	B
		T	E	E	T	H	E		N	O	T	I	C	E
T	R	E	A	D		C	O	L	O	R	E	D		
R	E	C	U	S	E		A	H	O	Y				
A	C	T		L	A	N	D	I	N	G	G	E	A	R
D	U	O		A	S	N	A	P		O	M	E	N	S
E	R	R		T	E	E	M	S		N	A	G	A	T

55

```
HOME  HAHA  SPAM
OVAL  ELON  OLDER
PETA  RIOT  LADLE
PRINTMEDIA  NEON
ELL  KENO  BLONDE
RADIOS  OBOE  DIG
SPAS  SAVEFACE
LADS  TERI
FILESUIT  LEAP
IPA  CEDE  COMPEL
NAUGHT  RAUL  IRA
INTO  OPENSEASON
TERRE  SNIT  LOBE
OMEGA  ACME  EDIT
ACER  SEER  SECS
```

56

```
SARA  SLIP  TRADE
OVAL  COMA  RIGID
CEDE  ROAR  AGENT
CRICKETMATCH
ESS  EWE  DIETARY
REHAB  RAINS  VIE
MAC  MSG  COPS
BUMBLEBEETUNA
PESO  APE  SIR
ALE  QUIRE  ADOPT
STRAUSS  JAR  NOR
BEETLEBAILEY
CACHE  LACY  NITS
ONION  EMTS  KNIT
STARS  SASS  SECS
```

57

```
RIP  AHAB  CABLES
ERR  NOTI  ABRAMS
SOONTELL  NOOGIE
UNFOLD  BRAVA
MOUSE  POOPEDPOP
ERS  RCA  BEAVERS
SEES  ATM  LIRAS
HOTHANDLE
ACTOR  PUN  WAFT
RAKEDIN  LAW  TRI
CLOSECALL  ESSEN
IRATE  CNOTES
AMAZON  GOODLAST
SAVEUS  INKY  KIA
PRESTO  TEES  EAR
```

58

```
BOCA  FRESH  SPED
OPAL  ROMEO  TOTO
LENO  EATAT  ARCH
TROUSERSLENGTH
SANDAL  LEE
LYE  DID  BRA
AREAS  FLEE  MOOS
BYAHAIRSBREADTH
CARS  BOUT  BOSSY
SNL  PEN  SIB
PAR  GETSAT
STUDIEDINDEPTH
SLAT  ALITO  MUTE
HINT  NICER  PRIM
EDGY  SEEME  ONCE
```

59

```
JEFF  MIMED  EBBS
OLDS  AROAR  PROW
EMIT  SALSA  SARI
COWHIDEGLOVES
PIUS  DONORS
ASS  SPEEDOS
SKIMP  VOW  PORK
WIDESCREENMOVIE
EDEN  RUN  ITALY
DOGTAGS  LES
SHADOW  DODO
HARDCOVERBOOK
AGUA  VITAL  ZINC
RUBY  ELATE  ELBA
PEAS  RESET  STAR
```

60

```
PLOP  CHAR  PLATE
RAVE  RARE  OASIS
EVER  INON  PIKES
PARKINGMETERS
SAG  AWAY
UMA  MEW  RECESS
MILESDAVIS  RACE
PALE  KIN  OGRE
ETAL  FEETOFCLAY
DAYSPA  OUR  EPA
RICH  TAP
RAILROADYARDS
HEINZ  ELMO  YEAH
EMOTE  DEMO  MENU
MUTES  ODOR  EDEN
```

61

A	R	E	S		M	A	G	M	A		O	K	R	A
T	E	X	T		D	W	E	E	B		N	E	U	F
T	A	P	E		P	A	R	T	Y		T	E	N	T
I	S	A	W	T	H	R	E	E	S	H	I	P	S	
R	O	N		O	D	D		S	A	M	S	O	N	
E	N	D	E	D		S	A	G		H	E	A	V	E
		T	A	D		M	U	G			K	E	G	
	A	W	A	Y	I	N	A	M	A	N	G	E	R	
I	R	A			P	E	Z		P	I	E			
T	R	I	C	E		W	E	B		X	E	N	O	N
S	O	T	H	A	T		U	K	E		U	N	E	
	W	H	I	T	E	C	H	R	I	S	T	M	A	S
O	K	E	D		M	O	U	N	T		A	B	U	T
W	E	R	E		P	U	G	E	T		F	E	T	E
E	Y	E	D		O	P	E	D	S		T	R	O	D

62

D	O	W		C	O	L	I	C		P	A	S	T	A
O	N	E		A	T	O	L	L		I	L	I	A	D
T	E	L	L	S	I	T	L	I	K	E	I	T	I	S
T	I	D	I	E	S		C	E	D	E				
E	D	E	N	S		A	S	H	Y		N	A	S	A
D	A	R	K		A	C	H	E		P	A	W	N	S
			A	S	T	O		T	O	T	A	L	S	
		T	A	L	K	S	T	U	R	K	E	Y		
D	R	A	P	E	S		G	R	E	Y				
Y	E	L	P	S		H	U	G	E		C	H	A	R
E	P	E	E		J	U	N	E		S	U	A	V	E
			A	T	O	M			C	U	R	V	E	S
L	A	Y	S	I	T	O	N	T	H	E	L	I	N	E
B	R	E	E	D		R	O	W	E	D		N	U	N
J	E	S	S	E		S	T	O	W	E		G	E	T

63

I	D	E	A		P	A	I	R		C	L	I	M	E
M	E	L	T		H	I	R	E		A	A	R	O	N
A	L	P	O		A	R	A	B		S	N	A	P	S
G	I	A	N	T	S	E	Q	U	O	I	A			
E	S	S		R	E	D		T	A	O	I	S	T	S
S	T	O	N	Y		A	S	S	T		Y	A	K	
		A	I	O	L	I		E	V	E	N	L	Y	
	G	R	A	N	D	E	N	T	R	A	N	C	E	
O	R	A	N	G	E		C	I	S	C	O			
H	I	P		N	E	E	D		U	S	A	G	E	
O	N	T	O	A	S	T		E	D	U		N	O	R
	G	R	E	A	T	P	U	M	P	K	I	N		
C	A	P	R	I		L	E	O	N		L	A	N	E
U	R	G	E	S		I	N	O	N		O	R	G	S
T	E	A	S	E		I	D	L	E		P	A	S	T

64

R	I	M		C	A	L	L	A		P	E	R	U
E	R	A		O	R	I	O	N		C	L	U	E	S
M	O	N		K	A	Z	O	O		L	U	R	E	S
O	N	T	H	E	B	A	N	D	W	A	G	O	N	
V	I	I	I		S	E	A	S		P	A	S		
E	C	S	T	A	S	Y			S	P	E	E	C	H
			D	O	M	E	D			G	A	T	E	
	T	O	C	O	N	C	L	U	S	I	O	N	S	
A	U	R	A		A	F	O	U	L					
G	R	I	N	D	S		S	P	L	O	T	C	H	
O	N	E		R	I	O	T			A	E	R	O	
	I	N	W	I	T	H	B	O	T	H	F	E	E	T
U	N	T	I	E		Y	A	H	O	O		T	A	B
S	T	E	P	S		E	L	I	A	S		E	S	E
C	O	D	E		S	L	O	T	S		R	E	D	

65

A	L	M	S		F	I	F	I		L	A	T	E	R
C	O	O	L		O	M	A	N		A	S	I	D	E
T	W	O	O	C	L	O	C	K		B	I	N	G	E
S	E	T	P	O	I	N	T		X	R	A	Y	E	D
				P	O	I		S	B	A				
G	R	O	P	E		T	A	C	O	T	R	U	C	K
L	A	R	E	D	O		L	A	X		A	S	H	E
U	Z	I	S		B	R	I	N	E		D	U	E	L
T	O	O	T		T	U	B		S	P	I	R	A	L
E	R	N	O	R	U	B	I	K		L	I	P	P	Y
			A	S	S		U	F	O					
N	O	Z	Z	L	E		S	N	O	W	P	E	A	S
E	T	A	I	L		P	O	G	O	S	T	I	C	K
S	O	N	N	Y		R	A	F	T		A	N	D	Y
T	H	E	S	E		O	P	U	S		S	E	C	Y

66

V	E	D	A	Y		I	M	A	M		S	O	M	E
E	R	I	C	A		R	E	N	O		Q	U	A	D
A	N	V	I	L		A	N	T	I		U	Z	I	S
L	O	A	D	E	D	Q	U	E	S	T	I	O	N	
			R	U	E			S	T	I	R			
A	S	T	O		C	I	O			B	E	A	R	D
S	P	E	C		O	R	A	C	L	E		W	A	R
P	A	C	K	E	D	A	S	U	I	T	C	A	S	E
I	C	H		T	E	N	E	T	S		A	R	T	S
C	E	S	T	A		S	E	T		T	E	A	S	
			V	I	C	E		E	T	C				
F	U	L	L	S	P	E	E	D	A	H	E	A	D	
R	O	S	A		P	O	L	L		L	A	T	T	E
O	X	E	N		A	X	I	S		E	L	T	O	N
B	Y	R	D		N	Y	S	E		S	L	E	P	T

67

```
P R O S . M A Z D A . . M E L .
J O L T . A L A R M . E M I R
S T E A M L O C O M O T I V E
. . S T O L E . P A L A T E S
T A T U M . . T I N E . T O T
M A R E . T W I T . R E N E
C H A T R O O M . S E E D E D
. . . T E A K E T T L E . . .
D E P E N D . S M A L L F R Y
E X E S . S U I T . T A K E
C P R . B E E P . R O B O T
A L G E B R A . B L A R E .
F O O T B A L L R E F E R E E
S I L O . S E E I N . E G A D
. T A N . E D G E D . L E T S
```

68

```
S C A M . C O D A . S T U B S
O H I O . A P E S . T E P E E
D U D S . M E M O . E A T E N
. M A T T E R O F R E C O R D
. E R A . . . E D U .
A N K A R A . C A R . P O L S
N O O N E . G A L A S . R A T
T R A N S P A R E N T T A P E
E S L . A L I A S . R I N S E
S E A T . A N T . G I N G E R
. . W O N . D O C . .
V A R I A B L E R A T E C D
E V E N T . A B I T . R E A L
T I N G E . S A N E . I D L E
O D D E R . T Y K E . N E E D
```

69

```
G A D . S K I D S . A B B A
E P E E . A N S E L . C L I P
L P G A . W E B E R . T A C T
C A R R O T A N D S T I C K
A L E . N O D . H I K E D
P L E A T . S O A P Y . T R I
. L A Y . B R R . F E E T
M R S P O T A T O H E A D .
C I A O . D A M . M O M
O R D . L A N A I . P A U L A
E R O D E . S T U . M I D
. O N I O N S K I N P A P E R
A R G O . A L I T O . F I L A
R E A D . P I L O T . T R O T
M D S E . S M O K E . E W E
```

70

```
S O R T . A P T E R . S T A B
O R E O . T E A R Y . L U L U
L E F T T H E P R E M I S E S
. A R E N A . B A G S .
G O B L I N S . O R C H A R D
U N T I E S . I K E . T U B A
S T U N S . B R A N . D I M
. G O A H E A D O F .
O A F . N C A A . T I T A N
T A O S . R I M . R E D E Y E
C A R P O O L . C O V E T E D
. S I N S . C R U E L .
Y O U G O T T H A T R I G H T
E U R O . I R A T E . T E A S
S T E T . C A P E R . Y E L P
```

71

```
K O A L A . I C A M E . D U C
E D S E L . N O L A N . R R R
N E E D L E P O I N T . E G O
. G A U L . E S S E N
N E W P O R T . D E B U S S Y
A T H E N S . A R A B I C
O H A R E . G L A R E . I B M
M A T T . S A T I N . F R A U
I N S . S E V E N . L A C K S
. M A H L E R . W A L L E T
D R Y C E L L . S E L L E R S
E U L E R . J E D I .
E P I . M A G I C S Q U A R E
D E N . A G E N T . U N D U E
S E E . N E O N S . E I D E R
```

72

```
J A C K . S O C A L . I P A D
U C L A . P A U L O . T O F U
S H U T T E R B U G . S C A T
T E E H E E . E M I S S A R Y
. L A D S . N O A H .
R E P E L . T A M . A D O P T
A L O E . T O R E U P . N E A
B L I N D S P O T S Y S T E M
B E N . R A I S I N . C A L M
I N T R O . T E E . M E S S Y
. T A I L . R U I N .
S L A P D A S H . S N A P T O
W I K I . S H A D E T R E E S
A P E D . S A V O R . I T A L
T O N S . O M E N S . O S S O
```

Solution: Medium Puzzles

73

T H I R D / O C T E T / N A M
Y A L I E / N O R G E / O L E
P U L P F I C T I O N / B U G
O N E S / S A Y / P A R M A
/ T R O W E L / K O A L A /
/ P E E L A N D S T I C K
M O N E T / M E E T / N E A
I R O N / P R I E S / T E L L
S E T / E R A S / T E R S E
T O U R N E Y S E E D S
/ P E R P S / V I S T A S
G I T M O / S I R / T R I P
I D O / B E E T L E J U I C E
L E I / E X P E L / E B S E N
T A T / S O A P Y / T E E M S

74

R A P S / P B A / S A G A
O R A L / C O L A / A E S O P
B E L A B O R T H E P O I N T
O N E T I M E / S P O U S E S
T A R / N E S S / I L L
A S S / T A C O / R O W
D E A L / A C E S / G U I D E
O U T O F T H E W A Y S P O T
W R I T E / O P E N / E A R S
N O T / S H O E / D I D
A T O / D R A T / R I M
H O T L I N E / E N C L A V E
A R R I V E D O N T H E D O T
L E A V E / G A T E / F I R E
L O P E / Y R S / T O Y S

75

F A M E / C A N I T / S C U D
L E A N / A M U S E / T U N E
A R M Y / C A R L A / A P S E
M A M A C A S S E L L I O T
E T A / H O S E / I N F E R
D E L H I / E M T / T A M
I N T R U D E / G E D S
P A P A H E M I N G W A Y
S U D S / R A P T U R E
P R O / H U M / A N G S T
A E R I E / S T E P / A P E
B A B Y F A C E N E L S O N
O R B S / U B O A T / A B U T
D E L E / S E N S E / M A S H
E D E N / S T E E R / A G E S

76

P S A L M / A L D A / S W I M
R E V U E / P O O L / C H A P
O M E G A / L O I T E R I N G
F I R S T R U N N E R U P
U S S / R I B
B E C A M E / T E N / D S T
A L O H A / S T A G / C I A O
S E C O N D I N C O M M A N D
I C K Y / I N T O / B O N E D
S T Y / M S G / C A N A R Y
P A T / I O U
T H I R D S T R I N G E R
S T E A D I E S T / M O O R E
E R A S / C L U E / P A R I S
W I R E / T I E R / S H E E T

77

C A P O N / S P I T / F L A N
A R R A Y / M A N O / A O N E
B O A T S / O R E O / U N T O
A M Y H E C K E R L I N G
L A S S / S E N T / L A S S O
D I S T I L L / H I M
C E S A R / S A T / B O N A
R A C H E L / D R A T C H
E T A S / A P E / A T S E A
E E R / F O R M A L S
K N E A D / A P S E / P A C T
C H A R L E S D A R N A Y
A F R O / E I R E / D I G U P
W O O L / A N O N / A M U S E
L E W D / P E R T / M O S E S

78

C O M A S / L S U / R A T
O R A T E / T O Y S / J U D O
S E C O N D H A N D / I N O N
T O S P A R E / C A B F A R E
T A N K / A F T E R
T U F F E T / E M E R Y
O P A L S / H E A L / L A T E
R O M A / C A P R I / U N I V
O N E S / A R M Y / A B O V E
H I N D U / S T E N O S
M E C C A / M O A T
E R R A N D S / P R E S E T S
S E E R / I N S T A N T T E A
A C E D / P I E S / D A T E S
S T D / S P A / S T U N S

Solution: Medium Puzzles

79

L	E	G	S		E	M	M	A		I	D	E	A
H	Y	D	R	A		M	O	A	T		R	U	G	S
A	R	I	E	S		I	S	N	T		O	K	O	K
H	I	T	A	H	O	L	E	I	N	O	N	E	
A	C	H	T		M	I	S	T		E	Y	I	N	G
			N	A	S	A		O	A	R		T	O	O
A	I	M	E	D		R	B	I		F	O	R	T	
D	R	A	W	A	R	O	Y	A	L	F	L	U	S	H
M	A	R	S		E	V	E		R	A	T	E	S	
I	N	K		B	Y	E		F	R	O	G			
T	I	T	L	E		R	E	E	K		S	H	A	D
	W	I	N	T	H	E	L	O	T	T	E	R	Y	
I	R	A	S		A	E	R	O		H	I	N	G	E
Q	U	I	Z		R	A	I	N		O	C	C	U	R
S	E	N	T		P	R	E	Y		U	K	E	S	

80

H	A	D		L	A	R	D		H	O	N	O	R
C	A	R	E		I	C	E	R		E	L	O	P	E
A	V	O	N		A	L	A	I		L	E	V	E	E
S	E	M	I		B	U	R	L	A	P	S	A	C	K
E	N	A	M	E	L		S	L	I	M				
			J	E	E	R		L	E	S	S	O	N	
M	O	T	E	L		O	G	L	E		I	T	N	O
A	R	E	A		P	L	E	A	D		L	I	E	U
S	E	E	N		E	L	M	S		A	K	R	O	N
T	O	S	S	E	S			S	E	L	F			
			L	O	S	E		S	E	L	E	C	T	
C	A	N	V	A	S	T	E	N	T		O	A	H	U
A	B	E	E	T		E	R	I	E		W	R	E	N
S	L	A	T	E		W	I	N	E		E	L	S	E
H	E	R	O	S		S	E	E	M		R	S	T	

81

W	A	S		T	E	D		B	A	H		M	A	R
E	M	T		A	X	E		O	R	E		E	M	U
B	E	E		V	A	N		B	M	W		D	E	L
F	R	E	N	E	M	Y		C	O	N	C	I	S	E
O	I	L	E	R	S		H	A	R		H	A	L	O
O	C	E	A	N		B	E	T	C	H	A	T	A	N
T	A	R	T		O	O	H		L	I	N	E	N	
		B	A	N	T	H	E	A	C	T				
	S	O	A	P	S		E	T	D		B	E	E	R
C	A	N	T	B	A	T	H	E		H	E	N	C	E
O	P	E	C		L	O	S		B	E	A	D	U	P
R	I	C	H	T	E	R		Q	U	E	T	Z	A	L
P	E	R		I	N	E		U	G	H		O	D	E
U	N	O		N	O	R		A	L	A		N	O	T
S	T	P		T	W	O		D	E	W		E	R	E

82

B	A	U	D	E	L	A	I	R	E		W	I	S	P
A	N	N	E	M	U	R	R	A	Y		A	M	O	R
R	I	P	E	O	L	D	A	G	E		R	A	R	E
Q	T	I	P		L	E	S		C	A	D	G	E	S
S	A	N	F	R	A	N		M	U	S	S	E	L	S
			R	O	B		B	O	P	S		F	O	P
F	A	M	I	L	Y	P	E	T	S		P	I	S	A
U	R	I	E	L		O	L	E		S	A	L	E	S
L	E	A	D		N	A	I	L	B	I	T	E	R	S
L	A	M		M	I	C	E		O	A	R			
S	C	I	T	E	C	H		F	E	M	O	R	A	L
C	O	H	E	R	E		T	R	I		N	A	N	A
O	D	E	S		J	A	S	O	N	B	I	G	G	S
P	E	A	L		O	R	A	N	G	E	Z	E	S	T
E	S	T	A		B	I	R	D	S	N	E	S	T	S

83

C	H	A	P		T	O	N	G	A		H	A	Z	E
A	I	D	A		I	V	O	R	Y		E	V	A	N
W	H	E	R	E	C	A	N	O	N	E	F	I	N	D
S	O	N	I	A		L	O	U		A	N	D	E	S
			E	M	U	S		N	A	T	E			
M	U	T	T	O	N		A	D	M	I	R	A	L	
A	S	I	A	N	S		R	E	I	N		D	E	I
D	U	A	L		A	I	R			B	A	G	S	
E	R	R		B	I	T	S		A	M	E	L	I	A
	P	A	L	E	T	T	E		N	I	N	E	T	Y
		I	G	O	R		B	A	N	D				
S	P	O	K	E		A	T	A		C	A	B	A	L
P	O	L	I	T	I	C	A	L	D	E	B	A	T	E
E	L	A	N		O	T	T	E	R		L	I	O	N
W	O	N	G		U	S	E	R	S		E	L	M	S

84

T	A	C	T		A	D	A	P	T	A	T	I	O	N
I	P	O	S		B	A	D	R	O	M	A	N	C	E
M	P	A	A		S	N	A	I	L	S	P	A	C	E
T	E	T	R	A		C	R	E	D	O		B	U	D
E	A	R		S	P	E	N	D		D	I	P	S	
B	L	O	T	S	A	T		D	I	R	T	Y		
O	T	O	H		Y	E	S	O	R	N	O			
W	O	M	E	N	S	A	R	M	Y	C	O	R	P	S
			S	P	U	M	O	N	I		P	O	R	T
	C	H	I	R	P		I	C	K	Y	P	O	O	
S	U	E	S		N	I	V	E	A		E	S	P	
A	R	A		P	L	A	N	O		T	I	B	E	T
H	A	R	P	O	O	N	E	R	S		M	U	C	H
I	T	S	A	S	E	C	R	E	T		O	R	C	A
B	E	T	S	Y	W	E	T	S	Y		K	N	O	T

Solution: Medium Puzzles

85

C	Z	A	R		R	A	K	E	D		P	O	D	S
H	I	F	I		O	L	I	V	E		A	L	O	T
E	T	A	L		Y	O	D	E	L		E	D	G	Y
F	I	R	E	M	A	N	D	R	I	L	L			
			O	L	E			E	L	A	T	E		
S	E	D	A	T	E		R	A	D	I	A	T	O	R
I	N	O	U	T		S	A	N	E			O	L	A
M	A	N	G	O	U	P	I	N	F	L	A	M	E	S
P	B	J		S	A	S	E			E	L	I	D	E
E	L	O	N	G	A	T	E		C	A	I	C	O	S
R	E	N	E	E				E	R	R				
		B	L	I	N	D	M	A	N	D	A	T	E	
O	A	H	U		L	E	A	P	T		A	M	O	R
F	O	U	L		L	A	T	T	E		Z	E	R	O
F	L	E	A		S	T	A	Y	S		E	X	E	S

86

S	A	T	R	A	P	S		O	F	F	W	E	G	O
E	Q	U	A	B	L	E		A	L	L	A	Y	E	D
R	U	S	S	I	A	N		T	A	I	L	E	N	D
V	A	C		T	I	D	Y		R	E	E	S	E	S
I	M	A	M		D	U	E	L	E	R	S			
C	A	L	M	S			P	L	U	G		A	C	T	I
E	R	O	D	E	D		P	L	U	S		H	A	T
D	I	O	C	E	S	E		U	N	C	U	R	L	S
O	N	S		S	T	Y	X			S	U	D	O	K	U
G	E	A	R		U	R	I	S		D	O	M	E	S
		R	O	D	E	N	T	S		N	O	D	E	
S	C	R	A	P	E		G	R	I	P		S	O	L
P	O	U	T	I	N	G		O	N	E	L	O	V	E
A	L	D	E	N	T	E		L	A	T	I	M	E	S
M	A	D	D	E	S	T		L	I	S	P	E	R	S

87

T	H	U	G	S		O	W	N	S		R	A	I	L
W	I	G	H	T		R	H	O	S		E	T	N	A
I	G	L	O	O		L	A	S	T		F	O	U	R
T	H	I	S	W	A	Y	T	O		C	O	N	I	C
		T	E	N		N	A	Z	A	R	E	T	H	
P	O	W	S		T	R	O	P	I	S	M			
A	A	H		R	E	N	T		M	U	E	S	L	I
P	H	I	N	E	A	S		T	B	A	R	N	U	M
A	U	G	U	S	T		O	V	A	L		I	R	A
		T	H	E	C	R	A	B		A	P	E	X	
R	H	E	T	O	R	I	C		W	O	E			
H	E	A	R	T		T	H	E	E	G	R	E	S	S
E	Y	R	E		G	R	I	M		R	I	L	K	E
T	Y	N	E		A	U	D	I		E	A	S	Y	A
T	A	S	S		P	S	S	T		S	L	A	Y	S

88

Q	U	A	R	T	E	R	S		A	D	J	U	S	T
U	N	D	E	R	T	O	W		C	R	U	S	O	E
A	M	E	S	I	O	W	A		T	A	K	E	I	N
G	O	N	E	O	N		P	R	E	T	E	N	S	E
M	O	O	T	S		F	O	O	D		B	E	E	T
I	R	I	S		P	A	U	L		V	O	T	E	S
R	E	D		S	I	X	T	Y	S	I	X			
E	D	S		P	E	P		P	I	T		F	A	B
		Z	A	R	A	G	O	Z	A		R	U	E	
L	A	B	O	R		P	U	L	E		W	E	D	S
O	R	E	O		D	E	N	Y		B	A	S	I	E
S	C	A	M	M	E	R	S		A	L	T	H	E	A
E	A	T	S	A	T		H	A	B	I	T	A	N	T
I	N	L	I	N	E		O	N	E	S	L	I	C	E
T	E	E	N	E	R		T	A	T	T	E	R	E	D

89

A	S	A	D	A		E	B	B		F	O	A	L	S
B	E	G	I	N		M	O	I		U	G	L	I	S
C	R	O	A	T		I	N	A	S	C	R	A	P	E
S	I	G	N	I	N	G	O	F	T	H	E			
		N	O	O	R		R	A	S		U	G	G	
		D	E	C	L	A	R	A	T	I	O	N	O	F
E	D	U		H	A	T	H		E	A	R	F	U	L
A	R	M	S		E	O	S		B	U	D	A		
R	A	P	I	D	S		D	E	E	M		R	A	T
T	W	O	D	O	L	L	A	R	B	I	L	L		
H	S	N		W	E	E		P	O	L	E			
		I	N	D	E	P	E	N	D	E	N	C	E	
W	H	I	T	E	S	W	A	N		E	R	I	C	A
T	A	M	E	R		A	C	T		W	A	N	T	S
A	T	O	M	S		Y	E	S		S	T	E	V	E

90

S	M	O	O	T	H	T	A	L	K		A	S	I	A
W	E	B	C	R	A	W	L	E	R		M	A	S	H
A	M	I	T	Y	V	I	L	L	E		O	B	O	E
B	E	T	A	M	A	X		A	M	P	U	L	L	A
		L	E	N		O	N	L	I	N	E	A	D	
B	A	S		A	T	E	D	I	R	T				
O	I	L	B	A	S	E	D		N	A	D	I	N	E
O	D	I	U	M		D	I	F		T	U	D	O	R
M	A	M	B	O	S		P	U	R	E	E	I	N	G
		B	E	E	F	A	L	O			G	O	O	
G	A	L	A	B	A	L	L		S	E	T			
O	R	I	G	A	M	I		P	A	R	O	L	E	D
T	U	T	U		I	N	F	I	N	I	T	I	V	E
A	L	U	M		S	C	I	E	N	C	E	L	A	B
D	E	P	P		T	H	E	S	E	A	S	O	N	S

Made in the USA
Middletown, DE
18 September 2023

38739134R00064